# MENTAL TOUGHNESS:

## THE SECRETS TO COMBAT OBSESSIVENESS, OVERTHINKING AND PROCRASTINATION LEARNING TO RESIST TEMPTATION, FIND YOUR COMFORT ZONE AND MINDFULNESS. PROGRAM YOUR MIND AND UPGRADE YOUR BRAIN

### BY DRAKE MOORE

# Table of Contents

# Introduction

If you need to be a triumphant trader, you need to learn to deal with extreme levels of stress. The markets are regularly confused and careless; they are, with no uncertainty, stressful. Your mind has constrained resources; when you feel stressed, an extraordinary extent of your resources are dedicated to dealing with the stress. You will, in general, have little energy left with which to focus on trading. It's a great deal like "packing" for an assessment in school. It accepts twice as long to learn material when you pack. Why? This is because you are increasingly stressed when you are attempting to gain under pressure.

When you're attempting to adapt to the ferocity of the markets, you are comparably trying to perform under pressure, and under not exactly ideal conditions. As you stretch yourself as far as possible, you go through mental and emotional energy. As you go through resources, there is minimal mental and emotional energy left for trading easily, effectively, and withholding your balance. You are increasingly inclined to freeze, and may ride an emotional thrill ride as you face winning and losing trades. You may even start to freeze and act unreasonably. It's fundamental for survival, to have the option to adapt to the consistently expanding requests of the markets.

Research has demonstrated that, if you can learn satisfactory approaches to adapt to stressful circumstances, events that generally produce stress need not create the stress reaction. You can build "mental toughness". The mentally extreme individual can persevere through abnormal amounts of stressful events, yet not feel stressed out. Adapting to stress is like weightlifting. If you lift beyond what your body can physically deal with, you can harm muscle tissue. Be that as it may, if you never stretch yourself as far as possible, you'll never build up new quality. Similarly, as you build up muscles step by step, you steadily build up your capacity to deal with stress.

The essential is to know how to deal with more exceptional levels of stress, yet additionally to discover time to recover. When it comes to the markets, for instance, it's enticing to trade throughout the day, at that point work late into the night back testing and evaluating new trading systems. Be that as it may, working indefatigably at such a pace will undoubtedly destroy you eventually. It is imperative to rest and recover. That doesn't mean recoiling from the markets, yet learning to deal with the weights of the markets at a continuous, reasonable pace.

By driving yourself to more prominent levels of test, and yet resting and recovering, you can build up mental toughness similarly that a weightlifter can deal with more noteworthy and more noteworthy physical burdens.

There are some essential advances that an individual can take to plan for stress and become changed following it. To begin with, as I've expressed ordinarily, it is fundamental to get, however much rest and to unwind as could be expected. Someone who does not get the proper amount of rest have restricted mental resources to adapt to day-to-day stressful events. Getting additional rest is significant. This may mean taking arranged rests during the day to restore. Try not to wrongly think that you'll be "passing up" a trading opportunity by taking a break.

# Chapter 1 Mental Thoughts

Mental toughness refers to the capability to manage, resist, and overcome any doubts, concerns, worries, and circumstances, which stop you from achieving your goals or succeeding at a particular task which you have set out to achieve.

It can also be seen as the ability to have that psychological edge which enables you to handle situations better than other people. This can be in a competition, training, or a lifestyle. It might be the ability to perform better at something or be more consistent and handle things better than your opponent. This can be measured in terms of how you remain focused, confident, determined, and in control when you are under a lot of pressure.

## Mental Toughness is a Habit and a Skill

Mental toughness gives you the skills that you need to compete with other people at the highest level and to achieve the best possible potential—whether in life or sport.

It is a skill that you develop, which allows you to push through any difficult circumstances without losing your confidence or failing to achieve your goals.

There are various questions that people ask regarding mental toughness, but the major one is whether it is a skill or a habit that one is born with.

The truth is that there are various assumptions that people make when it comes to mental toughness:

- Mentally tough people usually perform better when there is pressure every time.

- Since someone falls apart when faced with stressful situations, they will tend to fall apart whenever the situation arises again.

- Mental toughness is an inborn character.

- Either a person is mentally tough, or they aren't.

The truth is that mental toughness is a skill that you can develop with time. You have to practice over it for you to be good at it. Remember that this is a skill and that skills can be developed when you put your time to it.

Mental toughness is a skill that, just like any other skill out there, can be learned. And for you to become the best at any skill you possess, you need to make it a habit. When you make something a habit, you end up making it automatic, and you won't waste a lot of time thinking how the skill works out; instead, you will make it work out for you in a short time.

## The Importance of Mental Toughness in Life

Being mentally tough is a skill that will help you succeed as a person. So, let us look at the various reasons why you need to be mentally tough:

## 1. It Improves Your Confidence

Mentally tough people are very confident when it comes to what they do—whether in sports or their daily lives. According to studies, when your mental toughness improves, so does your confidence.

Confidence refers to a positive state of mind that allows you to have the ability to handle issues with the best outlook. When you have a proper mindset during any activity that you do, you will work at it better and with more confidence.

Whether you are working as a team member or as an individual, the only way that you can achieve your goals is to put your mind on the positive aspect of what you are doing and being able to understand what you can control or not.

Every situation usually comes with nervousness that even the best expert will experience time and time again. This nervousness is the main issue that leads to failure among people.

For you to get past this, you need to have a healthy mindset and possess mental skills with will be able to control emotions and thoughts

You need to make the goals, both short and long, your priority, and you will be able to focus on them and achieve them. When your goals are clear, you won't have the time to feel nervous at all. You will set yourself up for the ability to achieve maximum performance at any goal that you go after.

For you to be mentally prepared, you need first to improve your mental toughness.

## 2. Greater Life Satisfaction

When you build mental strength, you gain better self-acceptance. With self, acceptance comes self-improvement. When you improve your life, you get the chance to enjoy your life fully, and you are able to turn any challenges into opportunities for you to grow.

As you build your mental strength, you will be more satisfied with your life, and you will be able to enjoy life. This is because when you are mentally strong, you have the capacity to turn your challenges into excellent opportunities.

As the mental strength grows, you will be more confident in all that you do, and you will focus on your goals and go after them. Additionally, you come up with the best priorities that are aligned better with your beliefs in life.

## 3. You Perform Better

The best thing that you can do as a person is to perform better at your chores. Whether you are a business person or an entrepreneur, you are out to be at your highest potential when handling any task that comes your way.

When you improve your mental strength, you will be able to reach the greatest potential ever and make sure you achieve more than you ever imagined.

Better mental strength allows you to regulate your emotions, manage your thoughts, and be more productive. This means you can focus all your energy and effort towards things that will matter the most each day.

4.  You Become More Resilient

Well, it is a known fact that you cannot control everything that comes your way the way you wish to—some will make it hard for you to manage. On the other hand, what you can do is to respond better when you are faced with hard situations. When you have better mental strength, you will be able to handle any challenge that comes your way the best way possible.

Mental toughness isn't all about being strong when times are hard; instead, it is all about being able to have the mental capacity to handle situations that come your way.

Many people think that mental strength is only for hard times, but this is not true because you need to be mentally strong even when you are running typical situations in your life.

Remember, as your mental toughness improves, so does your capacity and confidence in handling any situation that comes your way.

5. It Encourages You

As an athlete or as a businessperson, you have doubts most of the time. You don't know whether you will succeed, or you will fail. When you have such doubts, you need to try and have faith while staying mentally tough. Remember, you have worked hard to develop the skills that make you mentally tough, and these skills are able to guarantee your success.

You need to trust this training when you go out to do something. Make sure you work with your teammates and other people so that you overcome any challenge that arises.

As you realize the need to remain mentally tough, your mental state becomes an asset in any task that you handle.

6. Improves Work Outcome

Studies show that mental toughness is a big factor when determining the outcomes in organizations. People who are mentally tough handle situations better than those that aren't tough at all. This is why it is better to have workers that are mentally tough on your team rather than have those that aren't.

Mentally tough people tend to deliver more work in such a short time, and they also work purposefully towards their goals each day. They are also more competitive, and this means better output, better attendance, and meeting deadlines.

7. More Work Satisfaction

Mentally tough people handle stress better and are less likely to develop mental problems when at work. They also handle stress well and are less prone to being bullied.

They are also more positive and will handle any work you throw at them the best way, regardless of the challenges that they will experience, they also respond better to adversity and change, which means that new ideas will be adopted better compared to people who are mentally weak.

They, therefore, are able to contribute to the organization in a better way compared to other people.

8. It Eliminates Self-doubt

Whether your goal is to finish the marathon, or to double revenue, you will usually experience self-doubt in one way or the other. Having doubts about the goals you have, and how to achieve them forms a common issue that people go through in their quest to attain something.

When you have the mental toughness that comes with training and practice, you will be able to eliminate any negative talk and go for your goal with better confidence.

9. It Gives You Motivation

Organizations around the world are faced with the problem of how to keep their workers motivated. However, mentally tough people have the capacity to stick to their goals and stay motivated. Mental toughness will help you focus on the goal and then go after it, even when you don't have the strength to do so.

You will be able to find your inner strength, especially when you feel unambitious, tired, and discouraged.

## 10. Helps You Stick to Your Values

Mentally strong people know good advice when they see it. When you are going after a goal, bad advice usually tends to drown out anything good that you are going after, which is why you need to be able to filter out the bad and go for the good.

When you are mentally tough, you have the capacity to rule out any bad criticisms and advice from the people that are around you, and you can focus on the good things.

You will be focused and follow your values to the latter, and this, in turn, helps you make the best decisions regardless of the feedback that you receive from the people that are around you.

## 11. Helps You Learn From Mistakes

Many people hide their mistakes, and this increases the probability that you will end up making the mistakes again sooner than you think. When you are mentally tough, you will be able to accept any responsibility that comes with making mistakes then be able to learn from those mistakes.

11. With every lesson that you learn, you will be moving closer to achieving your goal.

While mistakes lead to failure, and failure is the core ingredient in losing out on your goal, when you make a mistake, you need to learn to spring back. People that are mentally tough have high self-esteem and will be able to bounce back from failure better than before. Failure is not a reason to give up for these people; instead, it is a way to move closer to their success.

12. Helps You Manage Your Fears

When you step out of your comfort zone, you find it hard to do some things that you were used to. When you are mentally tough, you get the courage to face and handle your fears better. Strong people have the ability to tolerate high levels of discomfort and will be able to move forward.

# Chapter 2 Characteristics of Mentally Though People

All mentally tough people have developed specific characteristics that are helpful to how they think, react, and make important decisions. Studying these characteristics and making attempts to mimic the behaviors and thinking patterns is one sure way to reach your goal of mental toughness faster. Use it as a blueprint that can be used and reused at will. Over time, the process will become like second-nature. You will instantly know when you are falling back into old habits or behaviors and can correct the course.

## Ability to Make Non-Emotional Choices

Allowing an emotional state to dictate your decision-making process will skew your outcome in directions that are non-productive or harmful. No matter how much your small child wants to cross a busy street by themselves and offer a tantrum to try and force a decision in their favor, better sense usually prevails, and the child waits until a responsible person can help them navigate heavy traffic safely. Letting emotions drive the decision can have terrible consequences, depending on the situation. Learn to separate emotion from sensible, rational thoughts.

## See the reality of the situation

Raw emotions can paint colors onto a canvas, which are not truly a part of the landscape. Irrational fears, negative thoughts, and a generalized feeling of hopelessness can invade every time you are faced with having to make an emotionally laced decision. As difficult as it may seem, take time to calmly look at the situation with an eye for realism.

## Goal-Driven

Keeping your eye on the goal is an important part of the development of mental toughness and a standard characteristic of anyone that always seems to achieve everything they set out to do or attain. It is an admirable quality worth replicating as often as possible.

## Recognizing a dead-end road

Taking the wrong path or making incorrect decisions is a waste of valuable time, resources, and energy. The skills it takes to recognize a dead-end road before you take the plunge is priceless. Is it a road filled with potholes or other unsavory obstacles? Is there a smoother, more direct route available? Not every path in life need be a struggle. At times, the struggles experienced are due to poor decision-making. Step back and look at the big picture. Even a difficult hedge-maze is solvable by looking at it from above.

## Untethering from details

Details can keep you bogged down, much like the tethers that hold back a hot air balloon from its flight. It is important to address all the details but do not get hung up in the process. Keep pushing forward for positive results. Maintain flexibility to change things if it makes the process easier. Higher levels of success are possible if you refrain from boxing yourself into side compartments and hop down unnecessary rabbit holes. Keep your eye on the goal line.

## Keeping a finished vision in mind

Knowing you have completed a road trip is obvious once you have reached your desired destination. An important characteristic of those with mental toughness is the ability to keep the finished goal or vision in mind, no matter what mayhem and chaos happens. It sounds easier than when you are stuck in the situation. The skill of practically putting on blinders to avoid being affected by the emotions of others is one that will serve you well. Stay in the knowledge that reaching your goal often means making unpleasant decisions or ones that are not popular with everyone in your circle.

## Ability to Set Aside Stress and Emotion

Stress can get kicked into high gear during emotional situations and exchanges. Decision-making and solutions can become clouded when stress is in a peak amount. Become instantly tougher in mental processes by learning how to set stress and emotional entanglement aside. You need a clearing, devoid of pressure to have the best perspective on any given situation.

## Ability to Welcome Change and Remain Flexible

When companies downsize or restructure, employees are faced with job loss, and this can sometimes be devastating. A mentally strong person will seize the opportunity to improve their life by weighing all of their options. If a mentally strong person who had been considering a career change is suddenly faced with losing their job, he or she will take this time to develop their skill set, return to school, or polish their resume to make a career change.

## Refuse to Let Fear Hold Them Back

A mentally tough person does not let fear hold them back. Everyone must go through challenges in life, and it is how we view those challenges that can shape our lives for the better. Change is scary, but so is remaining in the same stagnant situation indefinitely. A mentally tough person would rather be scared for a short amount of time while they are going through a change in life than live in fear of the change, never improving or bettering their situation.

## Will Not Let Toxic People Affect Them

A toxic person is someone who ruins the environment or the atmosphere for those around them. The toxic person might be incredibly jealous, judgmental, or just negative overall. A toxic person is like the grown-up version of the playground bully: he or she has low self-esteem and is so unhappy with their own lives, so they are constantly trying to bring others down to their level. A mentally strong person realizes this and will do their best to see things from the toxic person's point of view if possible. A mentally strong person also realizes that the toxic person is unhappy, so he or she will not let the toxic opinions and attitude affect them and their work.

## Exert Assertiveness

A mentally strong person is assertive. They say what they mean, and they mean what they say. They know how to use concise language so that the meaning of their words is not mistaken and their intentions are not taken the wrong way. Mentally strong people know how to say no. They know that it's ok to take time to themselves, whether that means saying no to an invitation they don't want to accept or simply staying in on a Saturday night to recharge. Mentally strong people also know when to set boundaries.

## They are very confident

If you don't feel confident about yourself and your skills, you cannot expect someone else to feel confident about you. Real confidence is essential and not false bravado. People often tend to mask their insecurities by merely projecting confidence, instead of being confident. A confident person will always stand apart when compared to all those who are indecisive, doubtful, and skittish. Their confidence often inspires others as well.

## They are good at neutralizing toxic people

A mentally tough person can keep his or her emotions in check while confronting a toxic person. Their approach would often be rational. If you want to be mentally strong, then you should be able to identify negative emotions like anger and shouldn't let these feelings get the better of you.

## They can say no

If you want to reduce your chances of experiencing stress and depression, then learn to say "no." Saying "no" is, in fact, good for your mental health. All those who are mentally tough possess the self-esteem and the foresight that helps them say no. If you have trouble saying "no" to others, then you should start working on it immediately. Saying "no" not only helps you in avowing unnecessary burden, but it will also help you in prioritizing your work and cutting off toxic people from your life.

## They can embrace failure

Failures are very common, and everyone has their fair share of failures in their lives. Mentally tough people are capable of embracing their failures. No one can experience success without knowing what failure is. When you can acknowledge that you are on the wrong path, are aware of the mistakes you are making, and can embrace your failures, only then will you be able to achieve success.

## They exercise

Exercising can help you in finding mental, physical, and emotional stability. When you start exercising, you are not only improving your physical health, you are getting rid of negative emotions as well. Start exercising at least thrice a week and you will feel better about yourself. Your self-esteem will get a healthy boost when you can develop your physical image. A person who is mentally tough knows the importance of exercising and will make sure that they are getting their quota of exercise daily. The endorphin high that you experience after exercising can lend your perspective some much-needed positivity.

## They get sufficient sleep

Sleep is quite essential if you are trying to improve your mental toughness. While you are sleeping, your brain starts working on removing all the toxic proteins that are produced because of the neural activity that takes place while you are awake. Well, your brain can do this only when you are asleep.

## They are always positive

Reading news these days has become a sad affair. Mass killings, suicide bombings, violence, crippling economies, failing companies, and plenty of environmental mishaps. Phew, that is a lot of negativity to go through. In times like these, it is quite easy to give up on a positive attitude. A mentally tough person wouldn't worry about all that for a simple reason. He or she cannot control any of those things. However, their attitude is something that they can control, and that's what they would concentrate on. They wouldn't waste their energies on something that cannot be helped. Instead, try utilizing your energy to do something good, and it might be helpful.

Mental toughness isn't a quality that only a few are blessed with. You can achieve it with some effort.

# Chapter 3 Scientific Studies of Mentally Tough

Most scientists stand out in their career than others simply because they have a diehard mentality that is very tough at discovering something new. A scientist who is not interested in discovering something new will always need to depend on what is already existing, but the one who is inspired and spirited will always desire to invent something, he wants something new to give to the world, something that nobody has ever done.

From history, we have seen scientist who gave us what we are still using today, such as, the principle of developing the LED globe and electricity. Michael Faraday the man who discovered electricity based on a particular principle of electricity he found out through personal discovery, Thomas Edison, the man who discovered the electric bulb tried several times and failed but he never gave up and he ended up giving the world one of the greatest discoveries of man which principle is today the basis of LED electric bulb production. Again, one thing that is common among these men was mental strength, if Thomas Edison gave up his idea on electric bulb, then he would never have discovered it. Mental toughness is the ability to consistently stick to what you believe that is going to work based on experimenting when it comes to scientific discovery.

Many scientists continue to experiment on something until they see that it is going to work, if it doesn't work, they keep on trying until finally they get the result. At this level, this is the scientists' mental toughness, the believe in the positive result of the outcome of what they are inventing. We can also borrow the knowledge of the science way of thinking or mentality to develop the area of life which we found is near impossible to achieve, I'll rather believe that it is going to work, and I'll keep working at it until I get it right.

The only thing that makes it not working for now is simply because you have not gotten it right, and the only way you'll ever get it right is when you keep working it and keep on practicing and doing it till you get it right.

The story of Thomas Edison is very interesting, he kept on believing that his invention will work, he never doubted himself, at the point of giving up, he just discovered what was missing and when he did discovered it, the rest is history, he got it right at that moment, the pain and suffering over the failed attempts was forgotten and what he achieve was what no man ever did achieve, today Thomas Edison is one of the renowned scientist for his good works of discovering the electric bulb.

The difference is that these men continued consistently believing that what they are doing will work and it did work. You will not just believe but add what you are doing to what you believe. With the right believe system that 'it is going to work' and actually doing what you believe is what will give you the result not when you don't believe in what you are doing, that will not give you the right result.

Again a man said during the time of Aristotle, the great Greek philosopher, that man cannot fly, Aristotle opined rather that man will fly, he believed in what he said, but many people mocked him and in response they said to him "You ought to know that you are wrong, even the ostrich with wings cannot fly, why should you ever conceive in your mind that man without wings will fly?" and so nobody believe what he said.

But many years later, man is flying from country to country from one continent to the other and from earth to the moon and outer space. Actually those who usually believe have a better mental strength or toughness than others.

Mental toughness also has to do with what you believe, if you believe in something and you develop a passion for it, you work towards achieving it, you will definitely get that thing. For this has been the story of many people in time past.

# Chapter 4 Understanding Fear

Fear is nuclear fuel in a human activity reactor. It forces one to act in the way that no threats, persuasion, logical arguments or arguments work.

Fear is a powerful resource, proven in business more than once. Who does not know J? Welch, the one who, having become the head of General Electric, reformed the company, using the fear of employees to be dismissed? Of course, fear was not the only force in his managerial revolution, but one of the main ones. J. Welch was not afraid of change, resolutely got rid of indecisive managers, and introduced the now-famous principle of working with staff up or out. He received his nickname Neutron Jack for dismissing about 100,000 people from the company. The management method of J. Welch was compared with an iron hand in a velvet glove. In August 1984, Fortune magazine, making a rating of the most severe bosses of America, put Welch on the first line.

When subordinates are reliably protected from coarse and direct threats, the manager may use more subtle ways of instilling fear. How did, for example, the company Ohio Bell, do this? Here they simply showed a film to all employees, who modeled the future. In this imagined future, Congress intended to nationalize the telephone system, as it gradually went bankrupt and lost its ability to provide relevant services. As a result, a huge number of employees lost their jobs. The film ended with the text that the announcer read to the audience: "Full-time work for a full day's pay! This appeal would help save the company if many years ago, workers followed it." The company calculated that the increase in labor productivity after watching this film allowed it to increase its revenues by $ 29 million over three years. A good argument for using fear to increase business profitability!

So, if we decided to use the emotion of fear in business development, how can this be done correctly?

We know for sure that fear affects not only the psyche, but also the entire body, the work of the endocrine glands are activated, and adrenaline is released into the blood. A person can only follow two primitive instincts - to face danger and attack first or escape. Fear can be rational, justified (when we are dealing with a real threat) and irrational (neurotic). In any case, our body acts the same way. The development of a sense of fear (emotion) occurs in two neural paths that must function simultaneously. The neurons process information, it is with their help that the body's responses (reflexes) to external and internal stimuli are formed. The first path is responsible for generating the most important emotions, the reaction along this path occurs quickly, allowing us to almost immediately respond to signs of danger. On the second path, the reaction is slower but more accurate. It allows you to more accurately assess the circumstances and more correctly respond to danger.

Since fear is learned and remembered the response of an organism to a threat (existing or imaginary), it means that this reaction can be controlled and even prevented or neutralized.

However, as a manager who worked with professional boxers, once said: "Both the hero and the coward feel fear equally, but only the hero struggles with his fear and turns him into a desire to win." Add: it is developed emotional intelligence that turns fear into a victorious resource.

Fear: disassemble, understand, use

We learn to use emotions to increase the efficiency of our business. To begin, consider the typical "recommendation for use" for fear. Naturally, first for personal use.

Recommendation 1. Get rid of.

If it is necessary to free oneself from fear, then one of the most powerful means is the opposite action. There is an opportunity - do what you fear. Afraid of heights - jump with a parachute, afraid of negotiations - participate in them constantly! This is possible if you overcome yourself.

Another classic piece of advice is to laugh at your fears, make them funny and funny. An annoying (frightening) senior business partner can be thought of as a monument along which pigeon droppings flow, for example. An employee of the tax police will not be afraid if you present him in a rage running after you with a fly swatter, etc. It has been established that laughter has a startling effect not only on mental processes but also on physiological processes. It suppresses pain, as catecholamine and endorphins are released during laughter. The former prevents inflammation, the latter acts as morphine. Laughter reduces stress and its effects, reducing the concentration of stress hormones - norepinephrine, cortisol, and dopamine. And more importantly: the positive effect of laughter persists throughout the day!

Recommendation 2. Understand.

A thinking person is less afraid. He is simply ... not in a hurry to be afraid, he has a habit developed on his machine that he will first understand what is happening and whether there are serious reasons for concern. This removes all sorts of fear and other empty experiences.

Recommendation 3. Act.

Reasonable actions calm the one who is anxious and change the situation itself to a more prosperous one. In a dangerous situation it is important not to worry, but to act correctly. Remember, the movie "The Crew," the ship's commander, summarizes: "To stay here is to die. So, you need to take off, no matter how small the chances for this are!" The commander does not have the right to fear in a dangerous situation.

Recommendation 4. Recall all good.

Fear leaves when a successful, positive experience appears when a person has confidence that he is able to cope with difficulties, that he is a winner. Gather your positive experience and accumulate success, as the camel accumulates water in his hump. Useful in a particularly dry period.

Recommendation 5. Raise your own morale.

How do warriors raise morale before a battle? The battle cry "Hurray!" How do Tibetan monks lead themselves to a meditative state? Sing the mantra "om." Each of us can find words, phrases that drive away fear and change our state. For example:

✓ "I'll do it!"

✓ "Yes!"

✓ "I!"

✓ "We will rock you!"

✓ "Forward, forward, forward!"

You shouldn't sag under a changeable world, let it be better bent under us!

It is important to select phrases individually, exclusively for yourselves. They do not necessarily need speaking out loud, they will produce the same effect if they are spoken yourself. The phrase with a built-in melody that can be sung even more strongly. In personal stock, it is good to have several phrases for the same state. If one does not work, the other will work.

Look for your own verbal formulas that are perfect for you. Although if someone's ready-made phrase works for you, why refuse a gift? For example, the phrase "I am not a hundred dollar bill to please everyone" helped out and continues to help many.

Recommendation 6. Fantasize.

Sometimes fear arises from a collision with something new, unusual, incomprehensible. Everything new in one degree or another causes wariness, apprehension. This is how the instinct of self-preservation works. After all, the unknown can be fraught with danger or even a threat to life! Fantasy helps to cope with this. It is not known what to expect from the negotiations. Are you nervous? Imagine unfamiliar business partners in suits and ties in an unusual situation. Let in your imagination they suddenly take out shopping bags with rotten eggs and tomatoes and begin to throw them in your direction. And you dodge them dexterously ... Then you take out a baseball bat and start to beat those tomatoes back! Spin the absurdity of this situation to the limit, until you feel funny and easy. Humor, as we know, is the best cure for fear.

# Chapter 5 Mentally Stronger and Acting Tough

There is a significant difference between acting tough and being mentally strong. A controlling supervisor at work, an incredibly demanding boss, bossy co-worker, or even an aggressive customer might be masking their lack of mental toughness by putting up a façade of toughness. Acting might help in improving someone's success initially, but not forever. However, for how long can a person keep faking? Mental strength is essential in the long run, and it cannot be faked. A successful person didn't rise to the top by feigning toughness. Instead, their success is associated with their mental strength. The stronger they are, the higher are their chances to succeed. Grit and persistence are necessary to become a top performer in any avenue. Along with this, there needs to be a desire to keep improving.

### 1: Failure isn't an option. Or is it?

It is highly unlikely that you will always be successful. Failure is a part of achieving success. Striving for success is a healthy attitude, but if you start believing that you always need to succeed on the first attempt itself, you are setting yourself up for failure. A mentally tough person knows that failures are part and parcel of life. They would think of failure as a temporary setback that they need to overcome and with this positive attitude, they will be able to do so quite quickly. A person who is pretending to be tough will be of the opinion that a failure is never an option. This attitude can become quite problematic when things don't go their way.

A perfect example of this is in relationships. How many times have you asked a person out, only to be turned down? This is something that happens to everyone. How you respond to rejection, however, defines whether you are acting tough or truly mentally strong. If you are merely acting tough you won't accept being rejected. Instead, you will likely keep asking the person out over and over again, believing that they will eventually give in, and thus make you the winner. This might happen in movies from time to time. However, in real life, constantly bothering a person can get you into real trouble. In fact, it could result in that person taking a restraining order out on you, turning a simple failure into an absolute catastrophe.

When you are mentally tough you will respond in a very different way. Rather than refusing to take "no" for an answer you will accept the outcome and consider your options. You might ask around to see why you were rejected. Perhaps the person you asked out is in a relationship, or maybe they just broke up with someone and need some time alone. In these cases you might choose to bide your time and try again later. Or maybe the person doesn't know you well enough to accept your invitation. In this case you can invest the time and effort to get to know them better, thereby improving your chances later. It may, however, simply be that they aren't interested in you, in which case you can move on and look for love elsewhere, not letting this rejection affect you any more than it should.

## 2: Faking toughness to mask insecurities

When a person tries to act tough, he or she is trying on a fake persona that seems to say "Hey! Look at me! I am great!" The façade they put up is quite brittle, and it can crumble at any given point of time. That tough exterior is simply a tool to hide their insecurities. It is okay to have certain vulnerabilities; you are human after all. A mentally strong person is aware of his or her vulnerabilities and tries to work on fixing them instead of pretending that they don't exist. You will be able to progress if you try fixing any weaknesses instead of covering them up and then hoping that they will go away.

One of the most common signs that a person is acting tough is that they appear to be far more self-confident than a normal person would be. This is often seen in confrontational situations. Any time two people get into an argument that gets out of control you will inevitably hear one of them begin to boast about not being afraid to fight. The lines "You don't scare me" or "I know martial arts" or "I'm going to destroy you" often hide the truth, namely that the person is in fact terrified of getting into a fight because they know they would lose. Therefore, the axiom "The dog who barks the most bites the least" comes into play here.

Alternatively, a mentally strong person won't boast that they aren't afraid, nor will they proclaim any fighting abilities that they might have. In fact, a truly mentally strong person will gladly walk away from a confrontation whenever possible. This is especially true for anyone who is trained in fighting. Since they are confident in their abilities they don't have the need to impress anyone or prove themselves in any way. Instead, they keep their composure and dictate the course of events as a result.

### 3: The "I can do anything" attitude

Being self-confident is important. However, there is a fine line between being self-confident and being cocky or overconfident. Self-confidence will help you in tackling challenging situations, and overconfidence is your shortcut to disappointments and failures. Overestimating your abilities will leave you inadequately equipped for dealing with realities of lie and underestimating the time required for achieving your goals will lead to severe disappointments. Mental strength is about understanding where you stand and what your abilities are. It isn't about having a false sense of bravado that can crack under the slightest pressures. It is about understanding your skills and working hard for achieving the goals you have set for yourself.

Someone who claims to be able to do anything will likely take on tasks or projects that are beyond their abilities just to impress others. This can be especially true in the event that a person takes a job that they aren't suited for. Any job requires a certain level of experience, training and inherent ability. As a result, when a person lacks those things they will struggle and likely fail. A person who acts tough will hide their lack of skill sets with the boast that they can do anything, regardless of what it is. More often than not the result is disastrous, as the individual gets into a situation that they simply cannot handle.

Alternatively, a mentally strong person will reveal any concerns they have before taking on a job or a role that they feel they aren't qualified for. More often than not they will simply turn an offer down, citing their lack of experience as the reason for doing so. However, in the event that they accept the challenge they will seek out as much training and support as possible. This will help them to learn the skills they need in order to be successful in the task at hand. Additionally, by looking to others for support they can get real time solutions for the problems they face, thus enabling them to learn as they go without risking their success or the success of those relying on them.

### 4: Acting tough usually involves a lot of pride

Those who would want to be perceived as being tough always feel that they have something to prove to others. Their self-worth depends on what others think of them. It doesn't depend on their perception of themselves but on what the world thinks of them. An attitude like this can take a toll on the individual. If your happiness is dependent on someone else's opinion, then you can never be satisfied. Becoming mentally tough is all about learning to be humble and understanding your abilities. A person who is mentally strong won't hesitate in asking for help when the need arises. They won't let pride stop them from asking for help or admitting ignorance of something.

An example of this toxic pride can be found in a person's need to be better than everyone else. It is perfectly healthy and normal to be competitive, but only to a point. When a person is acting tough they take being competitive to a whole new level. In business, when a person absolutely needs to be first in sales, customer service results or any other area where performance can be measured it indicates that they are trying to prove a point, namely that they are the best. The need to prove this usually indicates the opposite, namely that the individual has low self esteem and is trying to compensate for it.

In contrast, someone who is mentally strong will appreciate the times when they are first in areas of measurable performance, such as sales, customer service, etc. However, they will never rely on that rank. Instead, they will usually attribute it to luck, the effort of the team or some other phenomenon that downplays their personal role in the success. Furthermore, they will be the first one to congratulate someone else who earns first place in those areas. Rather than envying another person's success they will celebrate it, offering true support and encouragement as a result.

5: "Tough" people tend to ignore their emotions

Concealing emotions is possible for a while. However, this isn't a viable idea in the long run. Ignoring feelings, in the long run, can cause a lot of damage to your mental health. Suppressed emotions tend to wiggle their way to the surface, eventually if not immediately. Not acknowledging your emotions and hoping that they will pass will not do you any good whatsoever. Being strong is all about understanding your emotions and acting rationally after considering those emotions. A person who is acting tough often believes that emotions are a sign of weakness and tends to ignore them. Only if you acknowledge what you feel, will you be able to get control over it.

This can often be seen in circumstances when a person has their feelings hurt, either by an event or a person, but they refuse to admit that they are adversely affected in any way. When a person acting tough is overlooked for a promotion they will likely proclaim that they didn't care about the promotion anyway. They may even go as far as to say that they are better off without it, and that it is something only an idiot would want. The problem with this is that they downplay important things in life, which leads to them not going the extra mile to achieve the goals they really want. Rather than using the pain of a situation as inspiration to improve, they simply hide the pain and remain stagnant.

Someone who is mentally tough will know the value of emotions, especially negative ones. By embracing the hurt of being passed over for a job or a promotion they find the will to improve their chances for the next opportunity that comes along. This can also be seen in athletes who use losing to spur them on in training so that they can run faster in the next race. The bottom line is that a mentally strong person will wear their heart on their sleeve so that they remain committed to doing whatever it takes to become successful.

## 6: They thrive on power

All those who act like they are tough, decide to do so because they like being perceived as powerful and in control. Due to this, they often tend to micromanage and boss others around. They also end up having unreasonable expectations and demands. A person who is mentally strong will like to focus their energy on controlling their thoughts and rationalizing their behavior instead of trying to control all other external factors.

This can be seen all too often in the world of retail where those who act tough fool themselves into positions of authority all the time. Any time someone who acts tough gets into a managerial position they turn their responsibility into power. They see their promotion as a prize, something they don't have to work for any more. Subsequently, they tend to become lazier and lazier, delegating more and more work to those under their supervision. Any time they make a decision that is questionable they fall back on their position, reminding people that they are the boss and that what they say goes.

A mentally strong person demonstrates a completely different character when they are in positions of authority. Rather than viewing a promotion as the prize they see it as a challenge, an opportunity to prove their worth all over again. The result is that they increase their efforts, working harder than ever to ensure their own success as well as the success of those under their supervision. Additionally, a mentally strong person welcomes other opinions and viewpoints, drawing from the vision and experience of others to ensure the best choices are made each and every time.

### 7: Acting tough = Tolerating pain

Becoming mentally tough isn't about tolerating pain. It is about learning from the pain you experience so that you don't have to go through the same thing again. A mentally strong person would like to focus on their overall growth and development and wouldn't treat their body like a machine.

It is not about having a tough exterior, but it is about having a healthy mind that doesn't waver easily. It is about developing mental strength and like any other exercise, it takes practice to improve mental strength.

Associating toughness with the ability to tolerate pain can also be seen in the workplace environment. Everyone goes through the scenario where they find themselves in a job that they begin to hate. The difference is what a person does when they come to the realization that they are fed up with their job and want a better one. Someone who acts tough will remain in the job they hate, believing that they are demonstrating strength by enduring their day to day suffering. In their eyes the longer they remain is the stronger they are. This means that rather than trying to improve their life they simply strive to tolerate the emotional pain their circumstances create.

Alternatively, a mentally strong person will recognize that pain is a sign that something is wrong and change is required. Needless to say, this isn't about the pain associated with growing and developing, such as weight training or developing a new skill, rather this is the pain associated with hitting your thumb with a hammer. You can choose to embrace the pain, or you can choose to stop hitting your thumb with a hammer. A mentally strong person will choose the second option, seeking a different job or a transfer that will end the pain they experience in the job they have. In the end, mentally strong people know that it's not about putting on a brave face when facing harmful situations, rather it's about avoiding harmful situations whenever possible.

# Chapter 6 Comfort Zone: What and Find the Comfort Zone

Many psychologists and scientists have used the word 'Comfort Zone' to mean many different things. Some say it is a time, a place, a space or a happening in a person's life where he is most comfortable. Comfort zone is all of this and more. It is a routine, a behavior, a habit, an activity and even an overall way of life that doesn't feel stressful. It is something that somehow gives a person mental and emotional security. It can also give a person a steady dose of happiness and a sense of contentment.

Given these definitions of a comfort zone, it does not sound like a really bad thing to have, does it? In fact, it sounds like something everyone wants to attain. A comfort zone is not really a bad thing. What really makes it awful is when a person is living in a comfort zone for too long.

As earlier mentioned, having a comfort zone is not bad. The thing that makes it unfavorable is when a person gets stuck in it for so long. Being stuck in the comfort zone for so long can make a person lazy, unmotivated and, often, frustrated. He also becomes less productive and his performance is not as great as it used to be.

Experts believe that there should be some stress or anxiety in a person's life. This kind of anxiety is called the 'Optimal Anxiety'. It is called as such because it is not too stressful that a person gets a nervous breakdown, yet it is not so easy that the person remains in his comfort zone. This kind of anxiety is when stress levels are just a bit higher than normal. It also has to be something that's just outside the comfort zone.

An example of an optimal stress for a student is his final exam. For employees, this can be likened to deadlines, performance evaluations, and job interviews. These kinds of stresses are not considered as life and death situations and keep people on their toes.

How Hard is It to Leave The Comfort Zone?

Have you ever tried breaking a 10 year habit like quitting smoking? If the answer is yes, the reason why leaving the comfort zone is hard will be very relatable. Comfort zones give people some form of happiness and contentment. It is very hard to leave because why would anyone want to leave something that makes him happy? Why would anyone risk going out and venturing into the world where he can be criticized, judged and ultimately FAIL? People do not like leaving their comfort zones because they have gotten used to it.

These are some of the other reasons why leaving the comfort zone is difficult:

1. It is easy – leaving something that takes very little effort and gives them comfort and security is not something that many people would do. People in the comfort zone see it as

something effortless that gives them all the satisfaction they crave. It provides them with security, satisfaction, and comfort. Leaving something that does not require a lot of effort on their part but yields an acceptable result can be tough.

2. They are afraid of the unknown – some people have this irrational fear of the unknown while others thrive in not knowing what will happen next. The people in the former situation are the ones who want to keep staying in their comfort zone because they are afraid of what will happen if they leave. They fear that venturing into the unknown will just bring chaos in their life. They stick to their comfort zone because they know what to do in that situation.

3. They are afraid of failure and getting rejected – people who stay in the comfort zone hate knowing that they have failed or that they are being rejected. They stay in the comfort zone because it is a state where they are always accepted. They almost never encounter failure when they are in the comfort zone. They use the comfort zone to be protected from potential failures and rejection like a security blanket.

4. It is predictable – some people thrive on routines and predictability and do not like to venture into something that can result to unpredictable outcomes. These routines and repetitive events provide comfort knowing that the next part of the 'story' of their lives will unfold just as they thought it

would. They dislike surprises and prefer things to happen as expected.

5. They feel like they have control – Many people who stay in the comfort zone think that they are taking control of their life by steering it away from potential disasters. They think that they would not be affected by any outside force if they just stick to their routine. The predictability once again feels desirable when people feel like they are losing control over the situation.

6. It is their form of normal – people who have been stuck in their comfort zone think that being in that situation means normal. They see other things as outside the box and unusual if they stray away from routine and predictability.

7. They dislike change – this is not to say that they are rigid and unbendable, but sometimes, people stay in their comfort zones simply because they hate changes. They like the idea that things will stay the same no matter what happens.

To reiterate, having a comfort zone is neither a good thing nor a bad thing. It is when a person remains in the comfort zone for too long that makes it awful. When people start becoming predictable and the excitement for life is gone, that's when it goes bad.

Getting out of the comfort zone has many benefits that far outweigh all the reasons why people do not want to leave it.

These benefits enrich and uplift the lives of anyone who take the leap and try the unknown.

# Chapter 7 How to Develop Habits and Set the Right Goals

Transformative habits are habits that you can employ in your everyday life that greatly aid growth. Adopting these habits and putting them to work in your life will put you on the right track to learn all there is to learn about something, to use it to its fullest, and to have an endlessly renewable interest in that subject.

Let's take a look at five transformative habits to keep when learning about something. You will want to write these down somewhere and make active strides toward integrating them into your daily routine!

1. Have a burning passion.

Go into the area of your interest with a passion for learning more about it. Let that passion carry you through the following steps. The more of a desire you have to know more about the subject and the more passionate you are about making this a part of your life, the more able you will be to face the bumps in the road.

People who perform the best are the people who love what they do. As a result of that love for what they do, they spend time and energy on it that everyone cheering them on will never see. Being devoted to your craft means more than simply being there when others can see you.

Take the lead, stay interested in your passion, and develop a passion for being the best at what you do.

2. Dream big.

The dreams we have for the future are what keep us working hard and running toward the horizon. Knowing that bigger and better things wait for us on the other side of the hurdles we face is a huge motivator that will help us to smash through those hurdles. There is nothing wrong with aiming for the stars with the goals that you set. They will only serve to help you.

As you find your dreams set on higher and higher goals, you will find that your acumen and your skill will continue to grow to support those goals. These things are connected and aspiring to be more does have a massive effect on your growth and development.

3. Be disciplined enough to do the mundane daily tasks.

Being dedicated to a craft, job, task, hobby, sport, etc., means more than being present for the parts that others will see. It means being there for more than just the fun parts, the glory, the excitement, and the joy. It means being there for the mundane, boring, tedious, grinding parts of it as well.

Honing a skill or a craft takes hours upon hours of practice, failure, adjustment, practice, failure, adjustment, practice... It goes on and on and you have to be ready to be there for that.

Self-discipline is a huge part of success in general. If you can have the control over yourself to do what needs to be done, when it needs to be done, you have a better chance of reaching unimaginable success.

4.  Be willing to be coached.

This is really important, so pay close attention: no one ever learned anything by acting like they already understood it. Be willing to be taught, be willing to learn, be willing to be corrected, be willing to be corrected, and always be on the lookout for new information on the subject of your interest.

There is no shortage of information on any topic you care to learn, no matter what it is. There is always a way to learn something you want to learn.

The most crucial point is to be willing to let someone teach you something. No one will think less of you for the questions you ask when learning your skills. If you let your pride get the better of you while you're learning your craft however, you will lose the respect of others, as well as their support. You will also be cutting yourself off at the knees as regards further improvement or honing of skills.

5.  Desire to be challenged.

Once you allow the challenging aspects of your craft to leave the area, you will lose interest. The best way to keep a muscle toned is to flex it, right? Think of your brain like the muscle it is. It needs to be worked and challenged and exercised in order to retain what it's learned its elasticity, and its ability to make things work!

Setting challenges and goals for yourself can give you things to work toward and it can keep your interest fresh! Remember that if there is no one with whom you can be in competition, you can always be in competition with your former self. There is always room for you to improve, and you should be eager to take that opportunity!

While we're on the subject of habits, there are some habits that could benefit you as someone who is looking to succeed. These are known as the habits of effective people. They are the habits that, if you keep them, they'll keep you on the right track and primed for success!

Let's take a look at those habits now.

1. Don't work yourself to death.

Striving for a sustainable lifestyle in which you can get all your work done, while still affording adequate time to take care of yourself is the most important thing.

If you can achieve this, you can ensure that you will be effective in the long term. This is a sustainable, recuperative, and rechargeable approach that allows you to take the time to do the things you personally need to do. Work is not your entire life and you would do well to treat it that way!

2. Be proactive.

Getting out ahead of things is always a great idea. Don't live your life hopping from urgent task to urgent task. Take the time to look ahead, see what will be needed in the near future, and account for it. This will leave you with fewer fires to put out, so to speak.

Have a clear vision for what your future should be and systematically work toward it to bring it into being!

3. Have your ending in mind from the start.

If you know where you're going, you can more accurately decide what you should be doing right now. Working right now, for the sake of working right now, is a waste of your time and your effort. You need to be sure that what you're doing will ultimately lead you where you want to go.

4. Prioritize

It can be easy to get snowed under with all the things that lay before you, ready to be done. In order to stave off that panic, the most efficient thing to do is prioritize. Find the things that need to come first and get a jump on them. As you systematically work through the things that need to get done right now, you will find yourself rolling into the future and setting up tasks that will need to be done later.

It's is imperative to be able to differentiate between urgent and important. Something could have a timestamp on it that tells you it needs to get done right now. However, it might be something that you can delegate, or it might not be important to you at all to complete. Be sure to factor this into your evaluation before you start working on it.

5.  Keep it fair.

When you're looking at the outcome of any arrangement that you're looking to make, don't try to come out on top. Coming out on top is a concept that movie villains use, and it doesn't actually do anyone any actual good. Through litigation and the trouble it takes to manipulate people into these situations, it's not even worth it in the end.

Go into partnerships and arrangements with the idea that they are mutually beneficial for both of you. If you can achieve that, you're doing great. Having an honest mindset when you go into business with someone is the best way to make sure you're both getting what you need from the business and that nothing will go awry.

6.  Hear before being heard.

Be sure that when you're being presented with a problem, you do your best to hear all there is to be said about it, from as many angles as are available. Once you have all the information, you can throw in your input and go from there to reach a resolution.

If you jump in too quickly in an effort to be heard, you could discourage someone from coming forward, you could muddy the perception of what occurred, it could stir the pot, and you might be missing out on pertinent information that could more easily help you to reach a resolution.

Be willing to hear others before insisting that you be heard.

7. Synergize.

This is a very popular word that is used throughout business and strategy. Let's breakdown what it is and what it means. Synergy is the interaction or cooperation of two or more assets to produce a combined result or effect that is greater than the sum of their individual parts or effects.

If you are able to put your sense of self-gratification aside so that you and your colleagues can share in the success, you will find the success to be even greater in measure for each individual involved.

## SMART Goals

Now that we've taken a look at the types of habits that can be the most beneficial to us in our goals, let's take a look at a method for setting goals! The goals that you set should meet five criteria to ensure that your focus is in the most economical and prudent place. Doing so will save you extra effort, and will help you to increase your chances of achieving the goals that you're setting over time.

Let's look at what SMART means!

Specific

Measurable

Attainable

Relevant

Time-based

We'll break this down by letter so you can see precisely what your goals should look like as you're setting them in your day-to-day, and in your long-term planning!

Specific

Having a nebulous goal can make it so much harder to achieve what you want. The more specific you are about the things you want to achieve, the better chance you have of achieving that goal.

You want to state what you'll do, and you want to use action words when you make those statements. For instance, if your whole goal is, "I want to be rich," there aren't a lot of specifics in there and the only verbs in the statement are "want," and "be." Those aren't particularly active words and this statement doesn't really fall into the category of specific.

Now, if you were to say something a little bit more, you could say something like, "I want to develop a new app that will generate $50k in its first year." This is very specific and features words that show action.

Now, once you set this over-arching goal, you can further break down the specifics of that goal. To do this, you can ask yourself some simple questions:

- "What do I want to achieve with this goal?"

- "Where do I want to do this?"

- "What will be my method?"

- "What is my timeline for this goal?"

- "Do I want to work with someone to achieve this? Who?"

- "Are there conditions or limitations with which I should be thinking at this stage?"

- "Why do I want to achieve this goal?"

These questions give you a really great base for understanding your goal, all the intricacies that will come with it, and it gets you into the right frame of mind to begin working on it.

Measurable

Our goals can be hard to quantify when we're in the beginning stages of them. If our ideas are too nebulous, it could be hard to tell if we've even been looking in the right places. Making sure your goal is measurable means taking the time to identify the things that you will see, hear, feel, and sense when you achieve your goal. It means taking the measurable elements of the goal you're setting and working with them.

For this aspect, you will want to gauge quantifiable results. While being happy is a great result for the achievement of a goal, it's hard to quantify. Try looking for something like, "I've gone from needing to walk with a cane, to being able to walk a 5k." These are quantifiable, measurable results that are tangible in nature.

Defining the physical specifications of the goal you're working on achieving is a great way to make it easier to visualize and achieve. You will know when you're on your way!

Attainable

This part of the process can be a little bit hard to swallow. Is the goal that you have in mind attainable? If it isn't, you owe it to yourself to be reasonable and state that it is not currently attainable. This doesn't need to mean that you can't work your way up to it eventually, but if you start to go right for it out of the gate without setting up the preliminary steps, you could be setting yourself up for heartache.

Make sure that, whatever you're shooting for, you're keeping in mind the real-world obstacles that stand between you and that goal!

Relevant

Is this goal something that is relevant to you and what you want for your life? Make sure that you're not setting goals based on the things that others want for your life. Your goals should be your own things that you personally want to accomplish.

Take a look at your motivations behind the goals you have and determine if they're something that is really relevant to you!

Timely

Give yourself a deadline! Remember Parkinson's Law! The time allotted for a task will inevitably be taken up by the things that are needed to complete it.

Put together a flexible timeline for your goal and all the tasks that will be relevant to that goal. Make sure that you make adjustments as you learn about how long things really take, and as you find out more things about your personal capabilities.

Keeping your timeline realistic can do wonders for your morale and it can help you to push harder to achieve the things that you want to achieve in your life. Being too tight with your timelines can set you up for a loss, and that wouldn't be fair either. Being too lenient on your timelines robs you of time that could be allotted for other, more involves tasks on the timeline.

Be sure you're being wise with your time and you will achieve your goals precisely when you mean to.

Setting Your SMART Goals

Be sure that when you're putting your goals together, you're focusing on the positive. If your goal is, "stop smoking," your attention will focus more on the smoking and on the negative.

Base your goal in the positive and you will find that it will bring more positive with it, and your focus will be on a healthier aspect of that goal. For instance, you could be working toward, "six months of nicotine-free living!"

Your focus is on being free of nicotine, on living, and on a precise timeline! Just like with the method of pulling yourself out of procrastination, you give yourself a short timeline. At the end of that timeline, you can reevaluate and keep the train rolling!

# Chapter 8 Managing Stress: Tips and Exercises to Reduce Stress

Stepping outside of your comfort zone and developing habits that push you towards your goals naturally come with some side effects, one of which is stress. We try to avoid stress like the plague, and that's partly because we understand more about the effects chronic stress can have on our bodies and mental health. However, not all stress is bad, and part of acquiring mental toughness is learning whether stress is helpful or harmful.

Nevertheless, before we get into that, we're going to look at what the stress response is and why it can be so detrimental.

## What Exactly Is Stress?

The definition of stress when the term was coined stated it is "the non-specific response of the body to any demand for change" (Selye, 1936). These responses can be mental, emotional, or physical. Think about all the things your mind and body do when you feel stressed. Your stomach may twist up in knots, anxiety begins to build, and all you can think about is whatever it is that's causing the stress. All of these (and more symptoms) culminate to form what we know to be the stress response. Once it gets going, it's very hard to return to a pre-stress state unless the stressor itself is gone.

There are three different types of stress, according to the American Psychological Association (n.d.).

### Acute Stress

The most common and frequently experienced type of stress, acute stress is brief and results from your response to a situation. For example, if one of your kids is sick and there's no one to stay home to take care of them, you may feel tense and irritable, which are both symptoms of acute stress. This type dissipates fairly quickly and goes away entirely once the stressor has been removed or dealt with.

### Episodic Acute Stress

This is the next level of acute stress, and you may have guessed by the name that it describes acute stress that happens regularly. If you frequently have tight deadlines at work, you may experience episodes of acute stress whenever the deadline is approaching that then go away once you've handed in your project.

However, this type of stress can also arise, no thanks to your mindset. If you worry a lot or are a perfectionist, you'll experience episodic acute stress. This may lead to stomach problems and emotional distress.

### Chronic Stress

Chronic stress is the new buzzword in health and psychology circles. The more our world evolves, the more stressors we're exposed to and, consequently, the more often we feel stressed. Any situation that is not fleeting or easily solved can lead to chronic stress because the stressor never goes away. This can lead to chronic illnesses — aside from stress —

that significantly impact your quality of life and shorten your lifespan.

## Tips and Exercises to Reduce Stress

Knowing the difference between good and bad stress means nothing if you continue to let the latter beat you up. Instead of allowing yourself to fall apart whenever you feel stress kicking in, turn to these tips so you can acknowledge it without letting it take over.

### Accept a Lack of Control

One of the biggest reasons why we feel stressed is that we can't accept that we aren't always in control. We have an obsession with micromanaging because we think that's how we will achieve success. In reality, this tendency to seek control in every situation makes us too rigid and unable to see alternative pathways. Then, when we run into a roadblock, stress comes crashing down because our perceived control has been thwarted.

The key to reducing stress is acknowledging that you're not in control. Instead of letting that idea scare you, let it relieve you of the burden. You're not in control, and that's okay. You don't have to manage your entire life, and that's a good thing. Once you step back and let life happen on its own, you can adjust better when situations change and make decisions from a place of logic instead of fear.

## Reduce the Stressors You CAN Control

While most aspects of life are not under your control, there are some things that you can influence. Wherever possible, reduce stress by eliminating your burden and learning to manage tasks better. If you have too much to do at work and it's causing you anxiety, learn to delegate. If you can make a change that will reduce the amount of stress in your life without sacrificing your goals, do it.

## Breathe

One of our physical reactions to stress is tension in the jaw, neck, and torso, which can affect our breathing patterns. When our body is deprived of oxygen, it's not happy and will tend to let us know. Combat both the physical and mental reactions by remembering to breathe and employing a breathing exercise when you feel overwhelmed. Counting backwards from 100 while slowly breathing in for one number and out for the next refocuses your brain and takes you out of the situation momentarily.

## Leave Room for Fun

Life is supposed to be enjoyable. Whenever possible, leave behind the worry, stress, anxiety, pressure, and seriousness and just let yourself have fun. Go to the park and watch the kids play, take a dip in a lake, or put on your absolute favorite movie and pay attention to every scene and line of dialogue. When we let stress take away our ability to enjoy ourselves, we're at the beginning of the end. No matter how bad things get, you're still alive, so let yourself appreciate that.

## Avoid Vices

You may be tempted to turn to cigarettes, alcohol, or drugs when under a lot of stress—don't. No matter how good you may feel after indulging, the underlying issue doesn't go away. Once you sober up, you'll be right back where you started only with a massive headache and a higher risk for lung cancer.

These vices also go against the tenets of mental toughness. Learning to be strong enough to face your issues head on will serve you well in all aspects of life, whether they're stressful or not.

## Take Care of Yourself

You can't take care of your life if you don't take care of yourself first. A healthy body and mind are better equipped to deal with life's challenges, so don't neglect either. If you sit on the couch eating junk food all the time, neither your body nor your mind will be in optimal states. The moment a stressor occurs, you'll be knocked down.

Physical and mental strength (and toughness) start on the inside, so once you've built a firm foundation of wellness within yourself, stress from external sources will have a harder time breaking through and getting to you.

Eat well — whatever that means for you. Diet fads come and go, but truly healthy foods never change, so stick to the basics. Get up and move during the day, especially if you feel stress coming on. Do whatever you need to do to prioritize your health because you have nothing without it.

## Know When to Ask for Help

You don't have to go through your entire life doing everything by yourself. That's not always a sign of strength. If you try to push through without asking for help, even when you really need it, that's foolhardier than anything. Know when you need help and don't be afraid to get it. Sometimes the stress in our lives is avoidable if we would only take the proper steps to better manage our time and resources. This goes along with reducing the stressors that you can control. Don't let your need to be a tower of strength be the cause of your collapse.

Beyond these tips, just remember that stress is psychological. It all starts in your mind. If you can learn to control your mind through mental toughness, you'll be able to address the root of the problem. Turn your mindset around so that you can turn your life around.

# Chapter 9 What Is Emotional Intelligence?

Emotional intelligence is the ability to recognize and understand your own emotions as well as the emotions of others. It has a variety of different definitions with no one definition being superior to the others. Some texts define emotional intelligence as having four fundamental parts which include: managing emotions, perceiving emotions, understanding emotions, and using emotions. Other texts consider emotional intelligence to be self-awareness, social awareness, relationship management, self-management, and emotional intelligence. Still more consider emotional intelligence to be composed of five parts; these five parts are social skills, self-awareness, self-regulation, motivation, and empathy. One thing that is agreed upon is that emotional intelligence consists of being both aware of your own self and your emotions as well as being conscious of the people around you and their emotions.

Emotional intelligence gives you the ability to differentiate between different emotions that you may experience and identify and label each one correctly. This skill is a very important skill for people to possess because understanding your own emotions and being able to differentiate between them gives you the opportunity to control your emotions and take steps to adjust them. For instance, if you notice that a given thing makes you depressed, you can take steps to counter that in advance to avoid or minimize this emotional response.

Understanding and being able to differentiate between the emotions, responses, and behaviors of others allows you to interact better with other people. This is very important because a great deal of our lives has to do with interaction with other people. You can benefit from this in almost every facet of your life. A salesman can understand body language, and facial expressions, and understands which statements a person may take offense.

The Ability to Listen to Your Emotions

Emotional intelligence is also the ability to listen to and adjust your thinking and behavior based on the information that your emotions are giving you.

For it to be a good idea, however, for you to listen to your emotions and be guided by them, you need to have the ability to keep your emotions in balance.

Your emotions need to be under control before it is okay to listen to them. It would not be wise for an overly emotional person to listen to and be guided by his or her emotions. Thus, you must be able first to identify your emotions, and then understand where your emotions are coming from and what triggers them. Is it an event from the past? Is it negative thoughts about your worthiness? Is it an overly inflated ego? It is important to understand whether your emotions are coming from the event or person that you are dealing with or something else before you judge your reaction.

Your emotions need to provide you with accurate information in order for you to be able to use them in a manner that is beneficial to you. Thus, you need to be in tune with your emotions and tune them up from time to time so that the information that they are presenting to you is useful and accurate and thus a good guide for your behavior.

Why Do You Need Emotional Intelligence?

Everyone needs to have emotional intelligence, and it can definitely make your life easier if you have a great deal of emotional intelligence. The ability to understand the way that others are thinking, feeling and may react as well as being in touch with your own emotions that are formed for the situations that are in can help you navigate through situations in daily life far more effectively and with greater ease than you would if you lacked this skill.

It is important for a person to understand how his or her emotions connect to his or her behavior. Emotions have a significant effect on how a person perceives things, and in turn how he or she reacts to it. If you do not understand and are not in control of your emotions, you may not understand the reason for your reaction. Many people never even bother to think about why they react a certain way to certain things. Your behavior directly relates to your reaction to certain stimuli.

Furthermore, the way in which other people react and behave toward you is directly correlated to the emotions that they feel when they are around you as well. So, it is best to be in tune to the so that you can do well. In fact, people with a high degree of emotional intelligence often manipulate other people's emotions to tilt situations in their favor.

When Do You Need Emotional Intelligence?

There are a significant number of situations in life when you need to have emotional intelligence so it would be wise to think that it is always good to have and utilize emotional intelligence. In fact, it can be argued that the only time that you do not need to have emotional intelligence is when you are sleeping...alone. This is because life is filled with interactions between other people and these interactions often involve emotions.

In Relationships

One of the most obvious times in which you can benefit from having emotional intelligence is in your personal relationships. Relationships are often filled with and even based on emotions.

Knowing when your spouse or significant other is happy, upset, or annoyed can help your relationship run a lot smoother, so does knowing the right thing to say and when to say it. Awkward people, people without adequate people skills often have a difficult time meeting people and thus forming relationships. If you have no clue what to say to the opposite sex, when or what they may find offensive, you may have a difficult time finding a mate, most cases are not this extreme, and most people do have some emotional intelligence; however, improving your emotional intelligence can help you to enjoy your relationships more, form more relationships and closer bonds with other people, feel less intimidated in social situations and network better with others.

At Work

Although it may not seem as though emotional intelligence comes into play as much at work, if there are other people around you at work, and these people are likely to experience emotions, then emotional intelligence can be a great asset to you in the workplace. In fact, emotional intelligence can help your workday go more smoothly, help you to get along with your coworkers better, get the people around you to look more favorably upon your ability to do your work and even get you a raise or a promotion that you have wanted for a long time.

The first time you use emotional intelligence at work is at the job interview itself. Since the interviewer may be seeing a number of different candidates, you do not only want to make sure that you impress him or her with your credentials and impressive resume, you also want to make sure that you do not rub the person the wrong way. Yes, catering to your interviewer's emotions is important if you want to land that job.

You know you need to be able to read signals and take hints in order to secure the position. But what does taking hints involve? Taking hints and reading signals involves identifying the emotions of the interviewer and acting according to what is pleasing to him or her. Or, it may mean realizing that this is not a person that you want to work with and that you need to look for another job. Either way, it is important for you to be in tune with the thoughts and feelings of the interviewer so that you can perform well or make a judgement call as to whether this is an environment that you can work in.

# Chapter 10 Improve Your Emotional Intelligence Strategies

Your emotional intelligence has absolutely nothing to do with how many books learning you have achieved in life. You can have extensive college degrees and be completely unintelligent with your emotional states, response, and triggers. Complete understanding and mastery of your emotions will place you at the top of the class when it comes to mental toughness.

## Understanding Emotional Controls

What is it about emotions that can hang us up when trying to cruise along in life? A major life-altering event is understandable, but what accounts for the brakes being slammed on life with emotions like depression, overwhelming sadness, jealousy, or rage? Are you doomed to being subjected to your daily ration of emotional energy? You can learn to adapt and work around emotions once you have a full understanding of what they are, where they come from, and how much control you can exercise.

## What causes an emotional response?

Negative emotions are typically tied to some of our deepest held beliefs about self-worth, life-satisfaction, and abandonment. Positive emotions tend to tie into already held memories of happiness, bliss, acceptance, and affection for others. As social creatures, humans are driven hard by emotions and emotional response to outside stimuli. Although many people define themselves as "loners" or solitary personalities, they are just as socially dependent on feeling confirmation and acceptance as anyone else. It is a part of human nature.

If you get devastating news, such as a death in the family or a serious medical diagnosis, the brain takes in this information, and the electrical activity hits full-tilt. Feeling of impending abandonment and not being able to see the person you love anymore can be temporarily overwhelming. Fear of death can also be a debilitating sensation, initially. The body responds by crashing in a way that causes overwhelming sadness and grief to take over. Getting news of a promotion at work or a new baby on the way can have the opposite effect. It can leave you feeling like you are walking on the clouds. It directly correlates to our deepest held beliefs of self or self-worth and can be a strong response.

## How to temporarily push emotions out of the picture

Receiving traumatic news of family illness, accident, or death cannot be completely pushed aside and should not be. It is moments like these that will consume your immediate thoughts and time with good reason. Other, lesser events such as losing your job or a breakup with a partner can be temporarily pushed off when you are trying to make it through a day at work or other activity. A few things to try are:

- Put in earbuds and listen to some uplifting, up-tempo music.

- Send your resume to ten awesome companies offering totally amazing jobs.

- Take yourself out to lunch to a nice, brightly lit café.

- Take a walk and reconnect with nature to regain a calm feeling.

- Avoid talking to others about the issue while emotions are raw.

## Identifying Emotional Triggers

Knowing what triggers certain emotions in you is one way to have the information you need to try and avoid situations that can become unpleasant. No one knows and understands your emotional makeup more than you and those closest to you. Unfortunately, you are one of the few that cares about your personal emotional health and well-being. Find out and obey your personal limits on triggering events, information, and subjecting yourself to situations that bring a negative emotional response. Pre-planning is often necessary.

# Sad and upsetting events

Hearing news that is upsetting or creates a lingering sadness has a way of completely disrupting your day. It never fails that someone gets upset about an opinion and it can ruin a perfectly good evening. Developing mental toughness should include disciplining yourself to withstand or avoid situations that can lead to triggering feelings of sadness or upset.

The best way to handle emotional triggers is to incorporate avoidance techniques. A few practical ways are:

- Bow out of conversations that are venturing into areas that trigger your emotional response.

- Do not watch the news if the news is upsetting to you.

- Keep conversations light with people you find irritating.

- Change the subject if someone is trying to trigger a response.

- Get your mind off it with the promise you can revisit it at a better time.

- If all else fails, walk away from a triggering event or conversation.

You may have to give these methods a try or come up with a few avoidance techniques of your own. At some point, you will be able to withstand things that used to trigger you as you develop more mental toughness.

## Giving and receiving anger

Anger is one emotion that needs to be completely brought under tight control. It is the one that can lead to violent actions brought to you or done by you to others. Rage can get out of control quickly and often with little reason. People have submitted reasons for murder being something as slight as getting an ugly look or being in a bad mood. Trivial reasons for such dastardly crimes are rare, but it happens. It demonstrates how quickly triggering anger can lead to an action that cannot be taken back. It is a lack of self-control that is the polar-opposite of mental strength and toughness.

Before lodging any complaints about the anger dished out to you daily, ask yourself if you are completely innocent of gifting people with an angry tirade now and again. Anger can manifest in many ways, even as passive-aggressive. A few ways we display anger are:

- "Flipping the bird" when someone cuts you off in traffic

- Giving someone the cold shoulder

- Yelling at someone for making a simple mistake

- Mumbling or cursing under your breath when you feel someone is taking too long at the check-out line

- Refusing to hold the elevator or door for someone that you have had a beef within the past

## Managing Negative Emotions

Any emotion you experience that interferes with what you are trying to accomplish can be considered negative. You may be besieged with joy that makes it difficult to be still. It is not a wonderful feeling at midnight when you need to be up early for work the next day. Anger, jealousy, insecurity, and any number of emotions that leave you feeling somewhat out of control are negative and need dealt with to experience peace and push towards mental toughness. Never let emotions make you feel tied down and controlled.

When experiencing a negative emotion, ask yourself the following questions:

- Where is the emotion coming from?

- Is it a situation or event you have any control over?

- Will it pass quickly?

- Do you need to change locations or activities for a few minutes or hours?

- Is there something you can do at the moment that will quickly change your state of emotions?

- Is there a pattern in the appearance, such as date, time of day, activity, or people?

- Is the negative emotion coming from you or transferring from someone else?

- Have you done anything in the past that has helped get rid of similar negative emotions?

## Combating sadness and depression

Overwhelming feelings of sadness and depression must be eliminated to consider yourself mentally tough. No matter how much you prepare yourself, things will happen that leave hurt, pain, and sadness. The death of a spouse, loss of a pet, a divorce, foreclosure, and many other life events can leave you feeling nothing short of shaken and sad. The danger of not dealing with sadness is that it can lead to depression long-term. A few ways to kick depression to the curb are:

- Give yourself a healthy time limit to begin getting out of the dumps.

- Begin a regular exercise routine and get plenty of sleep.

- Go see a friend and talk.

- Begin seeing a therapist if you have no one to talk to.

- See the doctor to make sure that there are no health problems behind the depression.

- Begin a hobby you find interesting.

- Do plenty of outdoor activities.

- Make sure your home has plenty of natural lighting.

- Avoid alcohol and drugs.

- Do not watch too much television or sit for long periods of time.

- Listen to soothing or uplifting music.

- Take a long shower or bubble bath.

- Get a professional massage.

## Pull the fuse on anger

Anger is the single most self-destructive negative emotion. It is imperative that you practice the best anger management techniques possible to pull the fuse if anger is a huge problem for you. One of the best ways to stop yourself in your tracks with anger is to look at a few videos of adults that throw public tantrums. Seeing the cringe-worthy actions and response from those around offers incentive to change your ways.

Always ask yourself why you are feeling so angry. What will it take to make the anger fade at that moment? How is your anger being received? Is there a better way to handle the situation?

## Balanced Emotional Health

Finding a healthy balance to your emotions is the preferable way for all people to live. Being too up or too down can be a miserable experience. Learning how to get and keep your emotions in balance is the perfect way to become stronger mentally. You will feel freer to make the decisions you need to and feel less derailed in all you do. Step off the roller coaster ride of emotional turmoil and experience a calmer, less chaotic daily routine. You will wonder how you ever made any progress this long living in an emotional swamp.

## Rolling with the punches

Acceptance, in some small measure, is another important part of developing greater control over your emotions and being mentally tough. Days will come that are filled with difficult events, information, and people. Flexibility in your schedule is helpful for the moments you switch to another activity, choose a different store to shop in, or spend time with loved ones. It is difficult to allow things to roll off your back if you are rigid in your demands and time. Develop the best methods of tolerance or avoidance you can use that work for your situation and lifestyle.

Developing and using a sense of humor is another great way to keep rolling when everything around you is going crazy. It is impossible to change the behavior of others, but you can make a point by placing a well-intentioned touch of humor that accentuates the ridiculous displays of unreasonable anger or unreasonable upset you are witnessing. It can stop the activity immediately. It could draw more anger if the person is way out there, so use your better judgment before attempting the humor route. You do not want to end up making the situation worse. If nothing else, you can walk into another area and have a laugh in private.

## Refusing to be ruled by emotions

Mental toughness means drawing a line on being ruled and drug around by your emotions or the emotional demonstrations of others. It is not difficult to completely lose control of your life by allowing emotional states to determine what you get done, where you go, and how limited your attempts to accomplish tasks will be. You will never be able to live life to your fullest potential until you have firm emotional control. How controlled are you by emotions? The following list is enlightening:

- You lose at least a half day of work one or two days each week due to personal emotional upheaval.

- Emotional arguments are a near daily occurrence in your home.

- Work stoppage from anger or arguing amongst employees is a frequent problem.

- You have given up on getting along with some people.

- People easily get under your skin.

- You feel tired and depressed daily.

- You feel angry constantly.

- You feel low energy and tired all the time.

- You worry and fret over the smallest details.

- You feel awkward in a group.

- You take statements too personally.

If any of these are a frequent problem, it might be time to begin working on getting better emotional control in your life.

# Traits of Mental Toughness

The unbeatable mind is strong and tough. It is resilient and relentless. It is determined, and it has the willpower and the drive to succeed. We all want an unbeatable mind and often get frustrated when we fall short of what we wanted to accomplish because we just could not stay focused and determined. Focus and determination are both products of having mental strength. These are some of the traits that the unbeatable mind people possess.

There are certain traits or characteristics that a person must possess in order to develop and establish mental toughness. Some of these traits are some important that if you do not possess them, you may need to take the time to develop these traits before you can hope to gain mental toughness.

Traits of the Unbeatable Mind

| |
|---|
| 1) Mental Competency |
| 2) Emotional Intelligence |
| 3) Resilience |
| 4) Willpower |
| 5) A Winner's Mind |
| 6) The Ability to Focus |

| |
|---|
| 7) They Surround Themselves with Other People Who Are Mentally Tough |
| 8) They Avoid Trying Too Hard to Go Against the Grain |
| 9) Expect Delayed Gratification |

Trait 1: Mental Competency

The first trait that you must possess to develop and sustain a certain level of mental toughness is mental competency. Having a sound and competent mind is the very first thing that you need to gain mental toughness. Mental competency is the ability to make sound judgement decisions. Thus, it is important to pay attention to and take care of your mental health before developing your mental competence. Taking care of your mental health is important to having the proper foundational environment for mental toughness to develop. Disorders such as bipolar disorder can cloud your judgement and make it very difficult for you to develop mental toughness.

Don't assume that your mental health and mental competency does not change when certain things in your life change. If you experience something such as a death or a severe emotional loss or you are going through post-partum depression, or you just entered menopause, take the time to go get your mental health checked out. This is a very important step to developing an unbeatable mind.

Trait 2: Emotional Intelligence

Emotional intelligence can be characterized as a type of emotional competency, similar to mental competency for the emotions. Emotional competency is the ability to identify, understand and control your own emotions while being able to identify and understand the emotions of others and adjust properly to these emotions.

Having a low level of emotional intelligence can make it very hard to succeed in areas of life that involve other people. For instance, a person who lacks emotional intelligence may find it hard to succeed in relationships due to the fact that he cannot identify and understand the emotions of potential dates and mates. This may lead to a significant amount of communication issues, a lack of enjoyment in the relationship, and the inability to form relationships altogether.

Moreover, having a low level of self-awareness can cause you to identify your own emotions improperly. You may fail to realize how you truly feel about a person, job, or issue because you were not in touch with your emotions. This can lead to less satisfaction in these areas of your life. A high level of emotional intelligence leads to self-awareness. A person who has mastered emotional intelligence skills is more likely to do things that lead to a higher level of satisfaction for him or her because he or she knows himself better.

People who excel in the area of emotional intelligence, however, may find it very easy to deal with people and gravitate toward people. The reason that these people tend to gravitate toward other people is that people have a tendency to reach to them well. There are two key factors which have a significant impact on the way in which people react to them, and these are 1) empathy and 2) and increased ability to communicate with others.

Empathy is the ability to understand the thoughts and feelings of another person. It is the ability to put yourself in their shoes so to speak. People who can empathize with others are more likely to make other people comfortable around them and feel relaxed. Furthermore, people tend to feel that the empathetic person cares more about their day or how they are doing than people who have not developed the skill to emphasize with others. This can lead to deeper connections. Thus, a person who has emotional intelligence and can emphasize with others is more like to have more positive strong connections with people than a person who does not know how to emphasize with others. And these strong connections are a support system upon which a person can build more mental toughness.

A person with emotional intelligence has better communication skills. Being able to understand other people's emotions and adjust accordingly aids in conversation skills tremendously. Understanding the emotions of others can keep you from saying things which are off-putting or offensive, both thing that can quickly end a conversation and convince the other person not to communicate as much with you in the future.

Communication skills are derived from not only having the ability to understand emotions and speech; it includes reading and understanding the use of body language, personalities and more. Much of communication is about listening. To be a good listener, you should learn to listen actively. Do not just stand there passively as a conversation is taking place, that a strong interest in the words that are being said. And be sure that you notice the facial expression and the body language. Hand gestures are also good for you to notice. Take in the whole scene and make a judgement with that in mind.

Trait 3: Resilience

Resilience is the cornerstone trait of mental toughness. In fact, many people consider resilience to be the definition of mental toughness. Resilience is the ability to persevere and persist even though the challenges that life brings you. It is the ability to dust yourself off after a setback and get back up and try again and again until you succeed. Resilience is what helps people to overcome the challenges and obstacles that they find when they start trying to achieve a certain goal.

There are a number of factors that make up resilience. One of the factors that play a role in resilience is possessing confidence in yourself. You must have confidence in order to succeed. Confidence is the belief that you can accomplish the goal that you have set out to accomplish, that you are good enough, and you deserve to achieve your goal. To achieve a lofty goal, you have to believe that you can.

Therefore, confidence is also the ability to limit and control your negative beliefs in yourself so that they do not outweigh the positive ones that are telling you that you can succeed. Throughout life, many people have formed a significant amount of negative beliefs about whether or not they can be something that they want to be or do something that they want to do. People may have been led to believe that they are limited by where they are from, how much money they have, their skin color, their looks and more. These beliefs tend to reside in the back of people's minds and stop them from believing that they can achieve certain goals in life and that they need to 'stay in their place' and dream they type of dreams that were made for someone like them. Peers, teachers, classmates and more may have discouraged a person from trying to achieve certain goals instead of encouraging the person to go after them. Therefore, resilience is the ability to get past these negative affirmations that have been placed in our minds, sometimes over the span of years, and to reprogram ourselves to see our chances of achieving these .goals in a more positive manner.

Trait 4: Willpower

People who are mentally tough have a significant amount of willpower. Willpower is the determination that is needed to do things such as lose 50 pounds, stop smoking, stick to an exercise routine and many other things in life.

Willpower is the ability to not give in to your negative desires. It is the ability to resist temptation in order to make changes in your life that will improve your life from its current state. In fact, a survey conducted by the American Psychological Association, it was found that the number 1 barrier that most people cited to making positive changes in their lives was the lack of willpower. Therefore, the most limiting factor that people face, according to the American Psychological Association is not the lack of money, lack of education, or the lack of time, it is the lack of the ability to resist negative temptation.

Willpower or lack thereof is one of the biggest hurdles that most people face. In order to quit smoking, you need to be able to withstand the urge to do so; but, the majority of people who try to quit smoking fail because their desire to quit is not as strong as their desire to smoke one more cigarette. Even though smokers who want to quit may be aware of all of the negative effects that smoking can have has on them such as a wide variety of health problems, high cost, stained teeth, walls and more, people still lack the sheer determination to quit the habit. A person who has mental toughness, however, is able to channel this determination and use it to effectively quit smoking. And willpower is the key to success in most of the goals that you have in life.

Trait 5: A Winner's Mind

Mentally tough people have the right mindset to achieve the task that they set out to achieve. They believe that they can do it and have a positive attitude and the likelihood that they will succeed. Having a winner's mind is about having the drive to push forward and not allowing yourself to take no for an answer. People with a winner's mind do have the willpower that is necessary to achieve the goals and dreams; in fact, this is something that many people with a winner's mind never even bother to call into question, unlike the rest of us.

Certain aspects are present within the winner's mind. A winner's mind is grateful for the things that he or she has. Being thankful for the things that you have allows you to have a positive attitude despite the things that you lack. A winner is glad for the everyday things that he or she was blessed with that will allow him or her to achieve his or her goals in life.

A winner's mind thinks positive thoughts. There are many people who allow their minds to be clogged with negative thoughts. This is something that is detrimental to their spirit, their mindset, and their likelihood of achieving the goals that they set out to accomplish. Winners concentrate on seeing things in a positive manner. In fact, winners try to surround themselves with a positive vibe and group of people altogether so that their mindset is connected to positivity.

In addition, a winner's mind is always ready and open to learn more and enhance the skills that the person possesses. Winners are constantly learning and developing and evolving in order to stay on top of their game.

Winners are always setting new goals. Once you reach one goal in life, a winner would not be satisfied to just sit back and be content that he or she had achieved that particular goal. Winner's tend to set new goals immediately after achieving one goal; the success of fulfilling one the first goal offers encouragement and confidence that the next goal that is set can be achieved as well. Winners also tend to set these goals in progression, or series, one right after the other, knocking them off like a to-do list. This helps to keep you motivated and striving to achieve more and more.

Trait 6: The Ability to Focus

We've all seen people who do not have a strong ability to focus and are easily distracted. In fact, there is a good chance that you are one of these people if you have not taken the time to try to develop your mental toughness. Mental strength improves your concentration. A significant number of exercises that are designed to help you improve your mental strength are focused on concentration.

Many high-performance athletes have tunnel vision when in their athletic performance mode so that they have a total and complete concentration that allows them to excel. This focus is necessary to make split-second decisions on how to deal with other players in order to come out on top. Many people who have never participated in these types of activities do not understand the type of focused zone these athletes get into and may have never honed their skills to get to total focus on the play at hand.

Trait 7: They Surround Themselves with Other People Who Are Mentally Tough

People with mental toughness tend to surround themselves with other people who are mentally tough. You often find that athletes and entertainers of a certain level tend to associate with each other, and you may have assumed that it is because they are celebrities or because they are highly paid. You may not realize that their work ethic may be part of the reason that they gravitate towards each other. Their careers are so demanding that other people may not understand this and may not agree with doing the same amount of work that they are willing to put in. These high-level performers keep each other on their toes and encourage each other.

And these people all possess a high degree of mental toughness which tends to feed off of each other. They can encourage each other to stay strong and work hard. They illustrate what mental toughness is in a given situation; they support each other and more.

It is rare that you see a person who seems to be strong mentally and emotionally closely associated with someone who is significantly weaker in these two categories. This is because, although the stronger one may rub off on and have an effect on the weaker one, the weaker one has an effect on the stronger one as well. The stronger one is being pulled down, and the weaker one is being pulled up toward a common average strength. This is often uncomfortable for both people. It can be frustrating for the stronger person who may often wonder why the weaker one fails to show as much willpower, determination, and drive, and it can be belittling for the weaker person who may experience insults and a condescending attitude from the other. Thus, it is beneficial for both people in associate more closely with someone on their level of mental strength.

This means that if you desire to develop your mental strength, you need to identify and surround yourself with people who possess mental strength as well. And you may have to eliminate or reduce association with some people who may keep you from reaching higher levels of mental strength.

Trait 8: They Avoid Trying Too Hard to Go Against the Grain

No, you should not always try to simply go with the flow and fit in. And the people known for having very high levels of emotional intelligence definitely stand out; however, there is nothing wrong with trying to fit in a little. Constantly trying to buck the system can get tiring and start to become frustrating.

In addition, this can place more stress and mental strain on a person. This takes up space in a person's minds and takes a good deal of his or her time that could have been spent on something else. Furthermore, trying to be different can start to take a toll on you emotionally. When working on improving emotional intelligence which is covered later in this book, you will learn to identify and understand other people's feelings and reactions and how to adjust to gain better responses from others.

Trait 9: Expect Delayed Gratification

People with mental strength do not need to reap immediate benefits for their work and actions. They are fine with the benefits coming in time for the work that they did and the time that they put in. Seeking instant gratification can keep you from achieving what you could have achieved if you understood that the payout for the work that you put in does not always come immediately. Sometimes, it may take years to see the fruits of your labor. It is still important to keep going in order to see the benefits of your work.

Honing your mental strength will allow you to see that rewards are not the only good thing that you receive from your hard labor. There is the pride of a job well done and accomplishing your goals. You can also enjoy helping others in some way. And the rewards for your hard labor will come in time.

# Chapter 11 Building Mental Strength

While telling a person to adopt the traits of the mentally strong is a good way to develop mental toughness, it may not always be enough. In a way it's a bit like telling a person that in order to be healthy you need to eat right, exercise, and get plenty of rest. Such advice is good and even correct, however it lacks a certain specificity that can leave a person feeling unsure of exactly what to do. Fortunately, there are several practices that can create a clear plan of how to achieve mental toughness. These practices are like the actual recipes and exercises needed in order to eat right and get plenty of exercise. By adopting these practices into your daily routine, you will begin to develop mental toughness in everything you do and in every environment you find yourself in.

Keep your emotions in check

The most important thing you can do in the quest for developing mental toughness is to keep your emotions in check. People who fail to take control of their emotions allow their emotions to control them. More often than not, this takes the form of people who are driven by rage, fear, or both. Whenever a person allows their emotions to control them, they allow their emotions to control their decisions, words, and actions. However, when you keep your emotions in check, you take control of your decisions, words, and actions, thereby taking control of your life overall.

In order to keep your emotions in check you have to learn to allow your emotions to subside before reacting to a situation. Therefore, instead of speaking when you are angry, or making a decision when you are frustrated, take a few minutes to allow your emotions to settle down. Take a moment to simply sit down, breathe deeply, and allow your energies to restore balance. Only when you feel calm and in control should you make your decision, speak your mind, or take any action.

Practice detachment

Another critical element for mental toughness is what is known as detachment. This is when you remove yourself emotionally from the particular situation that is going on around you. Even if the situation affects you directly, remaining detached is a very positive thing. The biggest benefit of detachment is that it prevents an emotional response to the situation at hand. This is particularly helpful when things are not going according to plan.

Practicing detachment requires a great deal of effort at first. After all, most people are programmed to feel emotionally attached to the events going on around them at any given time. One of the best ways to practice detachment is to tell yourself that the situation isn't permanent. What causes a person to feel fear and frustration when faced with a negative situation is that they feel the situation is permanent. When you realize that even the worst events are temporary, you avoid the negative emotional response they can create.

Another way to become detached is to determine the reason you feel attached to the situation in the first place. In the case that someone is saying or doing something to hurt your feelings understand that their words and actions are a reflection of them, not you. As long as you don't feed into their negativity you won't experience the pain they are trying to cause. This is true for anything you experience. By not feeding a negative situation or event with negative emotions you prevent that situation from connecting to you. This allows you to exist within a negative event without being affected by it.

Accept what is beyond your control

Acceptance is one of the cornerstones of mental toughness. This can take the form of accepting yourself for who you are and accepting others for who they are, but it can also take the form of accepting what is beyond your control. When you learn to accept the things you can't change, you rewrite how your mind reacts to every situation you encounter. The fact of the matter is that the majority of stress and anxiety felt by the average person is the result of not being able to change certain things. Once you learn to accept those things you can't change, you eliminate all of that harmful stress and anxiety permanently.

While accepting what is beyond your control will take a little practice, it is actually quite easy in nature. The trick is to simply ask yourself if you can do anything at all to change the situation at hand. If the answer is 'no,' simply let it go. Rather than wasting time and energy fretting about what you can't control adopt the mantra "It is what it is." This might seem careless at first, but after a while you will realize that it is a true sign of mental strength. By accepting what is beyond your control, you conserve your energy, thoughts, and time for those things you can affect, thereby making your efforts more effective and worthwhile.

Always be prepared

Another way to build mental toughness is to always be prepared. If you allow life to take you from one event to another you will feel lost, uncertain, and unprepared for the experiences you encounter. However, when you take the time to prepare yourself for what lies ahead, you will develop a sense of being in control of your situation at all times. There are two ways to be prepared, and they are equally important for developing mental toughness.

The first way to be prepared is to prepare your mind at the beginning of each and every day. This takes the form of you taking time in the morning to focus your mind on who you are, what you are capable of, and your outlook on life in general. Whether you refer to this time as mediation, contemplation, or daily affirmations, the basic principle is the same. You simply focus your mind on what you believe and the qualities you aspire to. This will keep you grounded in your ideals throughout the day, helping you to make the right choices regardless of what life throws your way.

The second way to always be prepared is to take the time to prepare yourself for the situation at hand. If you have to give a presentation, make sure to give yourself plenty of time to prepare for it. Go over the information you want to present, choose the materials you want to use, and even take the time to make sure you have the exact clothes you want to wear. When you go into a situation fully prepared, you increase your self-confidence, giving you an added edge. Additionally, you will eliminate the stress and anxiety that results from feeling unprepared.

Take the time to embrace success

One of the problems many negatively-minded people experience is that they never take the time to appreciate success when it comes their way. Sometimes they are too afraid of jinxing that success to actually recognize it. Most of the time, however, they are unable to embrace success because their mindset is simply too negative for such a positive action. Mentally strong people, by contrast, always take the time to embrace the successes that come their way. This serves to build their sense of confidence as well as their feeling of satisfaction with how things are going.

Next time you experience a success of any kind, make sure you take a moment to recognize it. You can make an external statement, such as going out for drinks, treating yourself to a nice lunch, or some similar expression of gratitude. Alternatively, you can simply take a quiet moment to reflect on the success and all the effort that went into making it happen. There is no right or wrong way to embrace success, you just need to find a way that works for you. The trick to embracing success is in not letting it go to your head. Rather than praising your efforts or actions, appreciate the fact that things went well. Also, be sure to appreciate those whose help contributed to your success.

Be happy with what you have

Contentment is another element that is critical for mental toughness. In order to develop contentment, you have to learn how to be happy with what you have. This doesn't mean that you eliminate ambition or the desire to achieve greater success, rather it means that you show gratitude for the positives that currently exist. After all, the only way you will be able to truly appreciate the fulfillment of your dreams is if you can first appreciate your life the way it is.

One example of this is learning to appreciate your job. This is true whether you like your job or not. Even if you hate your job and desperately want to find another one, always take the time to appreciate the fact that you have a job in the first place. The fact is that you could be jobless, which would create all sorts of problems in your life. So, even if you hate your job, learn to appreciate it for what it is. This goes for everything in your life. No matter how good or bad a thing is, always appreciate having it before striving to make a change.

Be happy with who you are

In addition to appreciating what you have you should always be happy with who you are. Again, this doesn't mean that you should settle for who you are and not try to improve your life, rather it means that you should learn to appreciate who you are at every moment. There will always be issues that you want to fix in your life, and things you know you could do better. The problem is that if you focus on the things that are wrong you will always see yourself in a negative light. However, when you learn to appreciate the good parts of your personality, you can pursue self-improvement with a sense of pride, hope, and optimism for who you will become as you begin to fulfill your true potential.

# Chapter 12 Rewarding Yourself

Celebrate your successes. Find humor in your failures – Sam Walton

Rewarding yourself from time to time for efforts taken is a good habit to adopt and a key part of the process that shouldn't be overlooked. Why you may wonder?

Because rewarding yourself motivates you and inspires you to continue taking action. By rewarding yourself, your mind will unconsciously start associating good feelings with finishing tasks. In other words, your mind will start relating positive rewards to each effort that you take. Do not allow your ego to run your life. You will find plenty of stories about rich people with deep regrets of not balancing their work with breaks. Work smarter, not harder. I sit back and smile when people declare they are the hardest workers (working 16-20 hours a day for active income), never sleep, and how much they love the grind. "Have fun," I tell them. I'll be the most efficient worker, I set up my businesses to grow while I sleep gaining passive income, and I will enjoy the grind from a place of want, not need. That's a long-term winning mindset.

Successful people reward themselves from time to time so that the effort feels worthwhile. You see it does you no good if you fail to reward yourself because as time goes by you may start getting a feeling of burnout and lack of desire to take action. This is especially true if you had to push yourself harder to take action. Therefore, coming up with a reward system is mandatory if you desire to be successful.

How then do you begin rewarding yourself? Rewarding yourself is fairly straightforward.

Method 1: Go out on a small trip

The first method that you should consider is that of taking yourself out. It doesn't matter how much you love the work you do. If you do it incessantly without taking even a small break, you will eventually burn out.

Going out on a small vacation is a good way to break off and renew your enthusiasm, energy and recharge your batteries . In addition, it helps you put things in focus.

There are lots of places you could go. You could try museums, malls, aquariums, open-air markets, the beach or any other place that is out of your normal routine. A good time to take small vacations like these is during weekdays when people are typically at work. During these times, these places are less crowded.

A key thing to keep in mind though is that you need to keep it short. Somewhere between two to four days is ideal. A short vacation will get rid of the fear that gropes you when you imagine of getting back to a mountain of work.

Method 2: Buying your favorite food

Another great way to reward yourself is treating yourself to your favorite food. When it comes to food, we all have our personal preferences of what we like best. What better way to reward all that discipline to get that work done than to simply go out and buy that food that you've craved for recently.

Thus, go out and grab that ice cream, drink a glass of wine, that pizza, or that cake. You could even cook your favorite meal if you wanted to. It doesn't matter what you prefer, you'll have to decide for yourself on this one. As long as it's something that you don't consume often so that it ends up feeling special to you once you take it.

Method 3: Reward yourself with self-care

Taking care of yourself is another way to reward your hard work and good behavior. We all love ourselves and would like to look and feel good. Making this part of your reward system can be an extremely powerful way to getting things done and becoming more self-disciplined.

There are countless ways of rewarding yourself with self-care. I will highlight a few ways so that you can get the idea and come up with unique ideas of your own. Some good ways of caring for yourself include:

- Going out and getting a manicure/pedicure

- Getting a new tattoo or piercing

- Taking a friend out for a meal and ordering whatever you desire on the menu

- Doing any activity that makes you feel free or similar to a child (e.g., amusement parks, concerts)

- Getting a massage at your favorite parlor

- Watching a great movie

Method 4: Take yourself out for some shopping

Another way that might work and make you feel good about yourself and strive to work better is to go out for some shopping. Although I wouldn't recommend reckless spending that would drive you to debt or make your broke, some of us just want our money to feel better than just numbers in the bank. You may want to compensate for that feeling by buying something.

For this reason, I will recommend one way for getting around the problem of overspending.

I recommend setting up a rewards account. This is like a savings account, only meant for buying rewards for yourself. Periodically, put some money into this account and reserve it for when you accomplish tasks successfully. Then, once you hit a significant milestone, you can dig into your rewards account and take yourself out for some shopping.

This will help you avoid overspending and still allow you to buy things for yourself as a way of making yourself feel good.

Method 5: Treat yourself to something fun but free

While buying yourself things like food, clothes, items and vacations are great ways for rewarding yourself, you don't have to make it all about money. All things considered, I would always advise that you seek ways of rewarding yourself that will involve little to no money. That way, you won't risk your financial freedom or stability. Always finding an excuse to spend money is not a great way to financial prosperity. That being said, here are a number of ways you can reward yourself and not spend money:

- Try going to a nice park/landmark in your town and enjoy nature

- Attend a free social event

- Play a video game at home

- Take a small nap

- Go out and take photos or videos.

As you can see, with a little creativity, you could come up with great ways to have fun but still avoid spending money.

All in all, this chapter has to some degree provided you with great ideas of rewarding yourself. Rewarding yourself is a great and fun part of cultivating self-discipline. Being mentally tough is good and this book has covered a huge part of doing that. However, what is even more important so that the good habits stick is to reward yourself consistently. It provides the much-needed incentive to keep pursuing your goals on your way to success.

# Chapter 13 Strategies to be Quiet and Strong in Every Situation

When you are faced by a serious life situation, the first reaction is always to panic not knowing that severe stress and anxiety can cause a complete mental meltdown. As a result, you can end developing long term health damage as well as reduce your ability to perform optimally when required to. Most of the world's top achievers, athletes, artists, and entrepreneurs could not have achieved their heights of success without mastering how to remain calm and collected when under pressure be it work or life-related. As a matter of fact, they have developed and maintain a certain psychological state of readiness and mental preparedness that helps them to accept situations much faster and address them calmly because they understand that situations van change abruptly but they do not define who they are or what the future holds for them. Circumstances and the people around you will often break you down. But if you keep your heart open to receive and give love, the mind focused and continue to move towards the right direction, it will always be easier for you to recover from the break downs and come back as a much stronger and more knowledgeable person. Here are tips on how to remain calm and collected at the height of pressure.

Accept the reality of the situation at hand

Through life, you can't discover peace. Instead of avoiding it, life spins every hour with unexpected modifications and takes every shift and experience as a growth challenge. Either it will offer you what you want, or the next stage will educate you. It does not guarantee any challenges and no hard work or noise before you find peace and good fortune in life. It implies to be in the midst and stay calm in your core. It's about letting your thoughts know how things should be. This isn't simple, of course; it's going to be a continuous fight. It's nevertheless infinitely simpler than fighting to adapt your life to some old delusion. It is also a trip that is endlessly more pleasing. There is peace, beauty and there is happiness when it works if you can separate from ancient beliefs. Honestly, life is too brief for you to go to war. Misappropriate expectations often lead to the greatest disappointments in our life. The first step towards happiness is to let go of unnecessary expectations. Come from a spirit of peace and acceptability and you can cope with and develop beyond virtually anything.

Understand that everything is temporary

Even when the storms are heavy, it eventually stops to rain. You also get a cure whenever you get hurt. Additionally, you are reminded every morning that light always comes after darkness, but choose to think that the night (dark moments in life) will continue forever. That's not going to happen because nothing lasts forever.

So if it's nice, appreciate it right now. It's not ever going to last. Don't care if things are bad, as it will never last. It doesn't just mean you can't laugh because life isn't simple at the time. It does not mean that you can't smile just because you're bothered by something. You get a fresh start and a fresh end at every time. Every second, you get a second opportunity. All you need is do the best you can.

Always push yourself to take another step forward no matter what you are going through

I am confident that about half the difference between good individuals and everybody else is sheer perseverance, this is after studying the lives of many successful individuals. We need to know the beauty of effort, patience, and perseverance in a society that wants fast outcomes. Be powerful, current and unwavering. Usually, the most beautiful smiles are those which have fought through tears. Because failures often ultimately lead to breakthroughs. Each error, heartbreak, and loss has its own answer, a subtle lesson for your performance and result from next time around. So it is you that is the most credible to predict your own future.

Enjoy life today, rather than just looking over it as it passes. Do not allow the few things out of control to interfere with the endless array of things you can control. The reality is that sometimes we all lose. The bigger reality is that we never have a single loss. Learn from your experiences and become wiser. Good things don't finally happen for those who wait: nice things come for those who remain patient as they work hard for what they most want in life, in good times and bad. This is about bravery. It is about being extremely scared and still proceeding to take the next step regardless.

Use positivity and do not let negativity bring you down

There might be no apparent reason today to be positive, but there is no need for a reason. Being always positive is a life strategy and not a response to something nice that might have happened. In fact, the ideal time to overly positive in life is when everything around seems negative and the world seems to be against you in every aspect. It is hard but achievable. Long-term happiness is not lack of issues, but the capacity to address them. Bring your consciousness to your own internal strength and positive position. You are responsible for how you respond in your lives to individuals and activities. You can either offer your life negative energy or choose to be positive by concentrating on the good things that really matter. So speak more about your blessings than today's issues. In other words, don't expect a favorable reason. Choose to be positive about your position, your opportunities and what you can do to get from one point to another. Look for ways to convey your favorable view rather than seeking reasons for being positive. Work to bring this vision to your lives and to enjoy the rewarding results you achieve.

Focus on achieving small fixes

Do not envision mountains in your mind. Don't attempt all at once to conquer the world. You unnecessarily make life difficult and frustrating if you look for instant gratification (large, fast fixes). Instead of making a small, beneficial investment in yourself at every time and the prizes will naturally follow. It's simple to discover a lot of small stuff when all is broken. Even the most important beneficial effort can create a major difference when nothing seems to be correct. Understand those times, when you are faced by the greatest adversity, are times when you encounter the greatest opportunities in life. If issues arise in every direction, it means that there is some great value somewhere waiting to be discovered and created. It's simple to get lulled into an indulgence routine when everything's well. How unbelievably capable and resourceful you maybe is simple to forget. Resolve to continue with small fixes daily. These little tweaks bring you to where you want to be in the long run. Every day, dense and thin, small steps, short leaps, and small fixes (small repetitive modifications) will take you places.

Look for something to appreciate no matter how small it may be

You may not have what you want and you may be very sad, but you can still enjoy more than enough at this time. Do not spoil what you have by wanting what you don't have; remember that what you got now was once just one of your desires. It is a sign of management and strength to remember that being positive in an adverse position is not naive. If you have so much to cry about and complain about, it is okay to mourn, but it is also important to smile and enjoy your life. So don't pray for the great miracles and forget to give thanks for the usual gifts in your life, simple but not that small. It may seem strange to be grateful for those ordinary events in your life, but it is precisely by being grateful that you can turn the ordinary into the uncommon and remain calm amidst pressure. Think of all the beauty around you, see it and smile. It is not gladness that makes us grateful at the end of the day, but gratitude that makes us happy. The most strong happiness activity here is to show gratitude for the excellent stuff you have.

Accord yourself the attention you deserve

It does not serve you to resist and ignore your own emotions and feelings. This leads to stress, disease, confusion, broken friendships, anger, and depression. Anyone who has had any of the above knows that those mental statements are terribly unhealthy and it is nearly impossible to escape them if you have the habit of self-disregard. You must confess to having spent too much of your life attempting to diminish yourself to a certain extent. Trying to be smaller in size, less sensitive, quieter, and less needy, have fewer opinions, and just be less of you simply because you were avoiding to push people away or to make feel like you are too much of a burden. You just wanted to fit in and make people like you by creating a certain good impression. You wanted to be needed.

For years, therefore, in order to please others, you have sacrificed yourself. You've endured for years. But you're tired of the pain and shrinking yourself. Good! It's not your job to make someone else's idea about a valuable human being shift who you are. You're valuable. Not because others believe you are, but because you breathe your own air, so you matter. Your ideas are important. Your emotions are important and your voice counts. And you must be who you are, and live your reality, with or without anybody's approval or authorization. Even if it turns the heads of individuals. Even though it does not make them easy. Even if they decide to quit, refuse to shrink your personality. Choose to give yourself the best in life, pursue your dreams and goals, and spare enough time for yourself. Above all, honor your emotions and feelings because self-care defines you. Once you take care of yourself and focus on being the best you can be, it will be easier for you to deal with people and situation under stressful conditions.

Always remember that everyone suffers and experience pain in life. But it is how people deal with adversities at the height of pressure that defines their level of success. Remaining calm during stressful situations helps you to make rational decisions and tap into your mental strength to ensure that you are not swayed by emotions. The key is to use your past life experiences to grow and move towards your achieve your goals a step at a time. When you remain calm and collected when under pressure you only give yourself the power to come up with the ideal solutions but also get to learn how to deal with future situations like the one you experienced. When you apply what you learn now in future plans, actions, and choices, you move forward and certain challenges also become easy to deal with. This is because, you took advantage of a stressful situation to learn, become stronger and wiser. It is not easy to remain calm under pressure because we are all humans and we are bound to react when our emotions are altered by situations. However, it is achievable and totally worth it in the end. Find what calms you down when stressed or under pressure and use it to remain motivated and positive to carry on with work.

# Conclusion

Successful people are mentally tough, to be successful in life, you have to be well prepared mentally, whether it is in your family, business, work or education. You have to have some level of mental development to be able to handle objection, the good and bad side of life.

Mental toughness therefore is very relevant and important to every individual. The world population keeps increasing, so many challenges coming up on daily basis. So, you get uncomfortable sometimes, because everything going around you tends to affect you, from politics, leadership, work, business, family etc. everyone seems to be involved and affected and then some things happen that affects you.

The truth you cannot deny and avoid is the fact that as long as we are all humans, everyone needs mental toughness. When the theory of survival of the fittest was propounded, other theories later emerged which postulates that some living things will have to struggle for their survival and it is those living things that were better adapted to changes in their environment that will be able to survive the changes in their environment. Therefore, you should know by now, that there will always be changes in our life and environment, the question is "how well will you be able to adapt to such changes?"

Secondly, ask yourself "have you developed that features that will enable you to carry out your own adaptation"?

Then it is very clear that one of the distinctive features you will need to develop is your level of mental toughness. Whether you like it or not, you need to develop yourself mentally and it will start somewhere, you may be scared right now on how to begin, let me tell you something, your waiting days are over, the simple truth now is that you have to get things started, taking actions is what you really need, and by the time you start with a single step that you decide to take now, you will sooner or later look back and see the distance you would have covered.

Don't wait any longer, take that bold step in the right direction, follow the basic principles and teachings as explained in this book, step by step and one at a time, always refer back to the contents and read to gain mastery of the various approaches and directives given in order to advance further.

The moment is now; get the right mentality to handle any situation you find yourself no matter what the circumstances. Be mentally tough and you will be victorious forever!

Let's hope it was informative and able to provide you with all of the tools you need to achieve your goals whatever it is that they may be. How amazing it must have been for you to realize that your mind is the primary determinant of where you are in life. It determines how quickly you move or how much you hesitate. Heck, it even determines how healthy you are. For these reasons, you need to ensure that your mind is continually tough to withstand the challenges that come about and to keep yourself moving ahead.

It helps when you work on yourself, using your abilities as a benchmark for future improvements, but you could also get inspiration from the works of great men and women that have achieved success in their lifetimes. See what they did when the odds were against them. See what happened when they listened to other people rather than to their own voices. Use their lives as lessons for your own life. You do not have to go through a lesson yourself to learn; other people make great illustrations too.

Lightning Source UK Ltd.
Milton Keynes UK
UKHW050045191120
373592UK00013B/276